The Poetry of Algernon Charles Swinburne

VOLUME XIV – POEMS & BALLADS (THIRD SERIES)

Algernon Charles Swinburne was born on April 5th, 1837, in London, into a wealthy Northumbrian family. He was educated at Eton and at Balliol College, Oxford, but did not complete a degree.

In 1860 Swinburne published two verse dramas but achieved his first literary success in 1865 with Atalanta in Calydon, written in the form of classical Greek tragedy. The following year "Poems and Ballads" brought him instant notoriety. He was now identified with "indecent" themes and the precept of art for art's sake.

Although he produced much after this success in general his popularity and critical reputation declined. The most important qualities of Swinburne's work are an intense lyricism, his intricately extended and evocative imagery, metrical virtuosity, rich use of assonance and alliteration, and bold, complex rhythms.

Swinburne's physical appearance was small, frail, and plagued by several other oddities of physique and temperament. Throughout the 1860s and 1870s he drank excessively and was prone to accidents that often left him bruised, bloody, or unconscious. Until his forties he suffered intermittent physical collapses that necessitated removal to his parents' home while he recovered.

Throughout his career Swinburne also published literary criticism of great worth. His deep knowledge of world literatures contributed to a critical style rich in quotation, allusion, and comparison. He is particularly noted for discerning studies of Elizabethan dramatists and of many English and French poets and novelists. As well he was a noted essayist and wrote two novels.

In 1879, Swinburne's friend and literary agent, Theodore Watts-Dunton, intervened during a time when Swinburne was dangerously ill. Watts-Dunton isolated Swinburne at a suburban home in Putney and gradually weaned him from alcohol, former companions and many other habits as well.

Much of his poetry in this period may be inferior but some individual poems are exceptional; "By the North Sea," "Evening on the Broads," "A Nympholept," "The Lake of Gaube," and "Neap-Tide."

Swinburne lived another thirty years with Watts-Dunton. He denied Swinburne's friends access to him, controlled the poet's money, and restricted his activities. It is often quoted that 'he saved the man but killed the poet'.

Swinburne died on April 10th, 1909 at the age of seventy-two.

Index of Contents

TO WILLIAM BELL SCOTT, POET AND PAINTER, I DEDICATE THESE POEMS IN MEMORY OF MANY YEARS

MARCH: AN ODE

1887

I

Ere frost-flower and snow-blossom faded and fell, and the splendour of winter had passed out of sight,
The ways of the woodlands were fairer and stranger than dreams that fulfil us in sleep with delight;

The breath of the mouths of the winds had hardened on tree-tops and branches that glittered and swayed
Such wonders and glories of blossom-like snow or of frost that outlightens all flowers till it fade
That the sea was not lovelier than here was the land, nor the night than the day, nor the day than the night,
Nor the winter sublimer with storm than the spring: such mirth had the madness and might in thee made,
March, master of winds, bright minstrel and marshal of storms that enkindle the season they smite.

II

And now that the rage of thy rapture is satiate with revel and ravin and spoil of the snow,
And the branches it brightened are broken, and shattered the tree-tops that only thy wrath could lay low,
How should not thy lovers rejoice in thee, leader and lord of the year that exults to be born
So strong in thy strength and so glad of thy gladness whose laughter puts winter and sorrow to scorn?
Thou hast shaken the snows from thy wings, and the frost on thy forehead is molten: thy lips are aglow
As a lover's that kindle with kissing, and earth, with her raiment and tresses yet wasted and torn,
Takes breath as she smiles in the grasp of thy passion to feel through her spirit the sense of thee flow.

III

Fain, fain would we see but again for an hour what the wind and the sun have dispelled and consumed,
Those full deep swan-soft feathers of snow with whose luminous burden the branches implumed
Hung heavily, curved as a half-bent bow, and fledged not as birds are, but petalled as flowers,
Each tree-top and branchlet a pinnacle jewelled and carved, or a fountain that shines as it showers,
But fixed as a fountain is fixed not, and wrought not to last till by time or by tempest entombed,
As a pinnacle carven and gilded of men: for the date of its doom is no more than an hour's,
One hour of the sun's when the warm wind wakes him to wither the snow-flowers that froze as they bloomed.

IV

As the sunshine quenches the snowshine; as April subdues thee, and yields up his kingdom to May;
So time overcomes the regret that is born of delight as it passes in passion away,
And leaves but a dream for desire to rejoice in or mourn for with tears or thanksgivings; but thou,
Bright god that art gone from us, maddest and gladdest of months, to what goal hast thou gone from us now?
For somewhere surely the storm of thy laughter that lightens, the beat of thy wings that play,
Must flame as a fire through the world, and the heavens that we know not rejoice in thee: surely thy brow
Hath lost not its radiance of empire, thy spirit the joy that impelled it on quest as for prey.

V

Are thy feet on the ways of the limitless waters, thy wings on the winds of the waste north sea?
Are the fires of the false north dawn over heavens where summer is stormful and strong like thee
Now bright in the sight of thine eyes? are the bastions of icebergs assailed by the blast of thy breath?
Is it March with the wild north world when April is waning? the word that the changed year saith,
Is it echoed to northward with rapture of passion reiterate from spirits triumphant as we
Whose hearts were uplift at the blast of thy clarions as men's rearisen from a sleep that was death
And kindled to life that was one with the world's and with thine? hast thou set not the whole world
free?

VI

For the breath of thy lips is freedom, and freedom's the sense of thy spirit, the sound of thy song,
Glad god of the north-east wind, whose heart is as high as the hands of thy kingdom are strong,
Thy kingdom whose empire is terror and joy, twin-featured and fruitful of births divine,
Days lit with the flame of the lamps of the flowers, and nights that are drunken with dew for wine,
And sleep not for joy of the stars that deepen and quicken, a denser and fierier throng,
And the world that thy breath bade whiten and tremble rejoices at heart as they strengthen and shine,
And earth gives thanks for the glory bequeathed her, and knows of thy reign that it wrought not wrong.

VII

Thy spirit is quenched not, albeit we behold not thy face in the crown of the steep sky's arch,
And the bold first buds of the whin wax golden, and witness arise of the thorn and the larch:
Wild April, enkindled to laughter and storm by the kiss of the wildest of winds that blow,
Calls loud on his brother for witness; his hands that were laden with blossom are sprinkled with snow,
And his lips breathe winter, and laugh, and relent; and the live woods feel not the frost's flame parch;
For the flame of the spring that consumes not but quickens is felt at the heart of the forest aglow,
And the sparks that enkindled and fed it were strewn from the hands of the gods of the winds of March.

THE COMMONWEAL

1887

I

Eight hundred years and twenty-one
Have shone and sunken since the land
Whose name is freedom bore such brand
As marks a captive, and the sun
Beheld her fettered hand.

II

But ere dark time had shed as rain
Or sown on sterile earth as seed
That bears no fruit save tare and weed
An age and half an age again,
She rose on Runnymede.

III

Out of the shadow, starlike still,
She rose up radiant in her right,
And spake, and put to fear and flight
The lawless rule of awless will
That pleads no right save might.

IV

Nor since hath England ever borne
The burden laid on subject lands,
The rule that curbs and binds all hands
Save one, and marks for servile scorn
The heads it bows and brands.

V

A commonweal arrayed and crowned
With gold and purple, girt with steel
At need, that foes must fear or feel,
We find her, as our fathers found,
Earth's lordliest commonweal.

VI

And now that fifty years are flown
Since in a maiden's hand the sign
Of empire that no seas confine
First as a star to seaward shone,
We see their record shine.

VII

A troubled record, foul and fair,
A simple record and serene,

Inscribes for praise a blameless queen,
For praise and blame an age of care
And change and ends unseen.

VIII

Hope, wide of eye and wild of wing,
Rose with the sundawn of a reign
Whose grace should make the rough ways plain,
And fill the worn old world with spring,
And heal its heart of pain.

IX

Peace was to be on earth; men's hope
Was holier than their fathers had,
Their wisdom not more wise than glad:
They saw the gates of promise ope,
And heard what love's lips bade.

X

Love armed with knowledge, winged and wise,
Should hush the wind of war, and see,
They said, the sun of days to be
Bring round beneath serener skies
A stormless jubilee.

XI

Time, in the darkness unbeholden
That hides him from the sight of fear
And lets but dreaming hope draw near,
Smiled and was sad to hear such golden
Strains hail the all-golden year.

XII

Strange clouds have risen between, and wild
Red stars of storm that lit the abyss
Wherein fierce fraud and violence kiss
And mock such promise as beguiled
The fiftieth year from this.

XIII

War upon war, change after change,
Hath shaken thrones and towers to dust,
And hopes austere and faiths august
Have watched in patience stern and strange
Men's works unjust and just.

XIV

As from some Alpine watch-tower's portal
Night, living yet, looks forth for dawn,
So from time's mistier mountain lawn
The spirit of man, in trust immortal,
Yearns toward a hope withdrawn.

XV

The morning comes not, yet the night
Wanes, and men's eyes win strength to see
Where twilight is, where light shall be
When conquered wrong and conquering right
Acclaim a world set free.

XVI

Calm as our mother-land, the mother
Of faith and freedom, pure and wise,
Keeps watch beneath unchangeful skies,
When hath she watched the woes of other
Strange lands with alien eyes?

XVII

Calm as she stands alone, what nation
Hath lacked an alms from English hands?
What exiles from what stricken lands
Have lacked the shelter of the station
Where higher than all she stands?

XVIII

Though time discrown and change dismantle
The pride of thrones and towers that frown,
How should they bring her glories down—
The sea cast round her like a mantle,
The sea-cloud like a crown?

XIX

The sea, divine as heaven and deathless,
Is hers, and none but only she
Hath learnt the sea's word, none but we
Her children hear in heart the breathless
Bright watchword of the sea.

XX

Heard not of others, or misheard
Of many a land for many a year,
The watchword Freedom fails not here
Of hearts that witness if the word
Find faith in England's ear.

XXI

She, first to love the light, and daughter
Incarnate of the northern dawn,
She, round whose feet the wild waves fawn
When all their wrath of warring water
Sounds like a babe's breath drawn,

XXII

How should not she best know, love best,
And best of all souls understand
The very soul of freedom, scanned
Far off, sought out in darkling quest
By men at heart unmanned?

XXIII

They climb and fall, ensnared, enshrouded,
By mists of words and toils they set

To take themselves, till fierce regret
Grows mad with shame, and all their clouded
Red skies hang sunless yet.

XXIV

But us the sun, not wholly risen
Nor equal now for all, illumes
With more of light than cloud that looms;
Of light that leads forth souls from prison
And breaks the seals of tombs.

XXV

Did not her breasts who reared us rear
Him who took heaven in hand, and weighed
Bright world with world in balance laid?
What Newton's might could make not clear
Hath Darwin's might not made?

XXVI

The forces of the dark dissolve,
The doorways of the dark are broken:
The word that casts out night is spoken,
And whence the springs of things evolve
Light born of night bears token.

XXVII

She, loving light for light's sake only,
And truth for only truth's, and song
For song's sake and the sea's, how long
Hath she not borne the world her lonely
Witness of right and wrong?

XXVIII

From light to light her eyes imperial
Turn, and require the further light,
More perfect than the sun's in sight,
Till star and sun seem all funereal
Lamps of the vaulted night.

XXIX

She gazes till the strenuous soul
Within the rapture of her eyes
Creates or bids awake, arise,
The light she looks for, pure and whole
And worshipped of the wise.

XXX

Such sons are hers, such radiant hands
Have borne abroad her lamp of old,
Such mouths of honey-dropping gold
Have sent across all seas and lands
Her fame as music rolled.

XXXI

As music made of rolling thunder
That hurls through heaven its heart sublime,
Its heart of joy, in charging chime,
So ring the songs that round and under
Her temple surge and climb.

XXXII

A temple not by men's hands builded,
But moulded of the spirit, and wrought
Of passion and imperious thought;
With light beyond all sunlight gilded,
Whereby the sun seems nought.

XXXIII

Thy shrine, our mother, seen for fairer
Than even thy natural face, made fair
With kisses of thine April air
Even now, when spring thy banner-bearer
Took up thy sign to bear;

XXXIV

Thine annual sign from heaven's own arch
Given of the sun's hand into thine,
To rear and cheer each wildwood shrine
But now laid waste by wild-winged March,
March, mad with wind like wine.

From all thy brightening downs whereon
The windy seaward whin-flower shows
Blossom whose pride strikes pale the rose
Forth is the golden watchword gone
Whereat the world's face glows.

Thy quickening woods rejoice and ring
Till earth seems glorious as the sea:
With yearning love too glad for glee
The world's heart quivers toward the spring
As all our hearts toward thee.

Thee, mother, thee, our queen, who givest
Assurance to the heavens most high
And earth whereon her bondsmen sigh
That by the sea's grace while thou livest
Hope shall not wholly die.

That while thy free folk hold the van
Of all men, and the sea-spray shed
As dew more heavenly on thy head
Keeps bright thy face in sight of man,
Man's pride shall drop not dead.

A pride more pure than humblest prayer,
More wise than wisdom born of doubt,

Girds for thy sake men's hearts about
With trust and triumph that despair
And fear may cast not out.

XL

Despair may wring men's hearts, and fear
Bow down their heads to kiss the dust,
Where patriot memories rot and rust,
And change makes faint a nation's cheer,
And faith yields up her trust.

XLI

Not here this year have true men known,
Not here this year may true men know,
That brand of shame-compelling woe
Which bids but brave men shrink or groan
And lays but honour low.

XLII

The strong spring wind blows notes of praise,
And hallowing pride of heart, and cheer
Unchanging, toward all true men here
Who hold the trust of ancient days
High as of old this year.

XLIII

The days that made thee great are dead;
The days that now must keep thee great
Lie not in keeping of thy fate;
In thine they lie, whose heart and head
Sustain thy charge of state.

XLIV

No state so proud, no pride so just,
The sun, through clouds at sunrise curled
Or clouds across the sunset whirled,
Hath sight of, nor has man such trust
As thine in all the world.

XLV

Each hour that sees the sunset's crest
Make bright thy shores ere day decline
Sees dawn the sun on shores of thine,
Sees west as east and east as west
On thee their sovereign shine.

XLVI

The sea's own heart must needs wax proud
To have borne the world a child like thee.
What birth of earth might ever be
Thy sister? Time, a wandering cloud,
Is sunshine on thy sea.

XLVII

Change mars not her; and thee, our mother,
What change that irks or moves thee mars?
What shock that shakes? what chance that jars?
Time gave thee, as he gave none other,
A station like a star's.

XLVIII

The storm that shrieks, the wind that wages
War with the wings of hopes that climb
Too high toward heaven in doubt sublime,
Assail not thee, approved of ages
The towering crown of time.

XLIX

Toward thee this year thy children turning
With souls uplift of changeless cheer
Salute with love that casts out fear,
With hearts for beacons round thee burning,
The token of this year.

L

With just and sacred jubilation
Let earth sound answer to the sea
For witness, blown on winds as free,
How England, how her crowning nation,
Acclaims this jubilee.

THE ARMADA

1588: 1888

I

I

England, mother born of seamen, daughter fostered of the sea,
Mother more beloved than all who bear not all their children free,
Reared and nursed and crowned and cherished by the sea-wind and the sun,
Sweetest land and strongest, face most fair and mightiest heart in one,
Stands not higher than when the centuries known of earth were less by three,
When the strength that struck the whole world pale fell back from hers undone.

II

At her feet were the heads of her foes bowed down, and the strengths of the storm of them stayed,
And the hearts that were touched not with mercy with terror were touched and amazed and affrayed:
Yea, hearts that had never been molten with pity were molten with fear as with flame,
And the priests of the Godhead whose temple is hell, and his heart is of iron and fire,
And the swordsmen that served and the seamen that sped them, whom peril could tame not or tire,
Were as foam on the winds of the waters of England which tempest can tire not or tame.

III

They were girded about with thunder, and lightning came forth of the rage of their strength,
And the measure that measures the wings of the storm was the breadth of their force and the length:
And the name of their might was Invincible, covered and clothed with the terror of God;
With his wrath were they winged, with his love were they fired, with the speed of his winds were they shod;
With his soul were they filled, in his trust were they comforted: grace was upon them as night,
And faith as the blackness of darkness: the fume of their balefires was fair in his sight,
The reek of them sweet as a savour of myrrh in his nostrils: the world that he made,
Theirs was it by gift of his servants: the wind, if they spake in his name, was afraid,
And the sun was a shadow before it, the stars were astonished with fear of it: fire
Went up to them, fed with men living, and lit of men's hands for a shrine or a pyre;

And the east and the west wind scattered their ashes abroad, that his name should be blest
Of the tribes of the chosen whose blessings are curses from uttermost east unto west.

II

I

Hell for Spain, and heaven for England,—God to God, and man to man,—
Met confronted, light with darkness, life with death: since time began,
Never earth nor sea beheld so great a stake before them set,
Save when Athens hurled back Asia from the lists wherein they met;
Never since the sands of ages through the glass of history ran
Saw the sun in heaven a lordlier day than this that lights us yet.

II

For the light that abides upon England, the glory that rests on her godlike name,
The pride that is love and the love that is faith, a perfume dissolved in flame,
Took fire from the dawn of the fierce July when fleets were scattered as foam
And squadrons as flakes of spray; when galleon and galliass that shadowed the sea
Were swept from her waves like shadows that pass with the clouds they fell from, and she
Laughed loud to the wind as it gave to her keeping the glories of Spain and Rome.

III

Three hundred summers have fallen as leaves by the storms in their season thinned,
Since northward the war-ships of Spain came sheer up the way of the south-west wind:
Where the citadel cliffs of England are flanked with bastions of serpentine,
Far off to the windward loomed their hulls, an hundred and twenty-nine,
All filled full of the war, full-fraught with battle and charged with bale;
Then store-ships weighted with cannon; and all were an hundred and fifty sail.
The measureless menace of darkness anhungered with hope to prevail upon light,
The shadow of death made substance, the present and visible spirit of night,
Came, shaped as a waxing or waning moon that rose with the fall of day,
To the channel where couches the Lion in guard of the gate of the lustrous bay.
Fair England, sweet as the sea that shields her, and pure as the sea from stain,
Smiled, hearing hardly for scorn that stirred her the menace of saintly Spain.

III

I

"They that ride over ocean wide with hempen bridle and horse of tree,"
How shall they in the darkening day of wrath and anguish and fear go free?

How shall these that have curbed the seas not feel his bridle who made the sea?

God shall bow them and break them now: for what is man in the Lord God's sight?
Fear shall shake them, and shame shall break, and all the noon of their pride be night:
These that sinned shall the ravening wind of doom bring under, and judgment smite.

England broke from her neck the yoke, and rent the fetter, and mocked the rod:
Shrines of old that she decked with gold she turned to dust, to the dust she trod:
What is she, that the wind and sea should fight beside her, and war with God?

Lo, the cloud of his ships that crowd her channel's inlet with storm sublime,
Darker far than the tempests are that sweep the skies of her northmost clime;
Huge and dense as the walls that fence the secret darkness of unknown time.

Mast on mast as a tower goes past, and sail by sail as a cloud's wing spread;
Fleet by fleet, as the throngs whose feet keep time with death in his dance of dread;
Galleons dark as the helmsman's bark of old that ferried to hell the dead.

Squadrons proud as their lords, and loud with tramp of soldiers and chant of priests;
Slaves there told by the thousandfold, made fast in bondage as herded beasts;
Lords and slaves that the sweet free waves shall feed on, satiate with funeral feasts.

Nay, not so shall it be, they know; their priests have said it; can priesthood lie?
God shall keep them, their God shall sleep not: peril and evil shall pass them by:
Nay, for these are his children; seas and winds shall bid not his children die.

II

So they boast them, the monstrous host whose menace mocks at the dawn: and here
They that wait at the wild sea's gate, and watch the darkness of doom draw near,
How shall they in their evil day sustain the strength of their hearts for fear?

Full July in the fervent sky sets forth her twentieth of changing morns:
Winds fall mild that of late waxed wild: no presage whispers or wails or warns:
Far to west on the bland sea's breast a sailing crescent uprears her horns.

Seven wide miles the serene sea smiles between them stretching fromrim to rim:
Soft they shine, but a darker sign should bid not hope or belief wax dim:
God's are these men, and not the sea's: their trust is set not on her but him.

God's? but who is the God whereto the prayers and incense of these men rise?
What is he, that the wind and sea should fear him, quelled by his sunbright eyes?
What, that men should return again, and hail him Lord of the servile skies?

Hell's own flame at his heavenly name leaps higher and laughs, and its gulfs rejoice:
Plague and death from his baneful breath take life and lighten, and praise his choice:
Chosen are they to devour for prey the tribes that hear not and fear his voice.

Ay, but we that the wind and sea gird round with shelter of storms and waves
Know not him that ye worship, grim as dreams that quicken from dead men's graves:
God is one with the sea, the sun, the land that nursed us, the love that saves.

Love whose heart is in ours, and part of all things noble and all things fair;
Sweet and free as the circling sea, sublime and kind as the fostering air;
Pure of shame as is England's name, whose crowns to come are as crowns that were.

IV

I

But the Lord of darkness, the God whose love is a flaming fire,
The master whose mercy fulfils wide hell till its torturers tire,
He shall surely have heed of his servants who serve him for love, not hire.

They shall fetter the wing of the wind whose pinions are plumed with foam:
For now shall thy horn be exalted, and now shall thy bolt strike home;
Yea, now shall thy kingdom come, Lord God of the priests of Rome.

They shall cast thy curb on the waters, and bridle the waves of the sea:
They shall say to her, Peace, be still: and stillness and peace shall be:
And the winds and the storms shall hear them, and tremble, and worship thee.

Thy breath shall darken the morning, and wither the mounting sun;
And the daysprings, frozen and fettered, shall know thee, and cease to run;
The heart of the world shall feel thee, and die, and thy will be done.

The spirit of man that would sound thee, and search out causes of things,
Shall shrink and subside and praise thee: and wisdom, with plume-plucked wings,
Shall cower at thy feet and confess thee, that none may fathom thy springs.

The fountains of song that await but the wind of an April to be
To burst the bonds of the winter, and speak with the sound of a sea,
The blast of thy mouth shall quench them: and song shall be only of thee.

The days that are dead shall quicken, the seasons that were shall return;
And the streets and the pastures of England, the woods that burgeon and yearn,
Shall be whitened with ashes of women and children and men that burn.

For the mother shall burn with the babe sprung forth of her womb in fire,
And bride with bridegroom, and brother with sister, and son with sire;
And the noise of the flames shall be sweet in thine ears as the sound of a lyre.

Yea, so shall thy kingdom be stablished, and so shall the signs of it be:
And the world shall know, and the wind shall speak, and the sun shall see,

That these are the works of thy servants, whose works bear witness to thee.

II

But the dusk of the day falls fruitless, whose light should have lit them on:
Sails flash through the gloom to shoreward, eclipsed as the sun that shone:
And the west wind wakes with dawn, and the hope that was here is gone.

Around they wheel and around, two knots to the Spaniard's one,
The wind-swift warriors of England, who shoot as with shafts of the sun,
With fourfold shots for the Spaniard's, that spare not till day be done.

And the wind with the sundown sharpens, and hurtles the ships to the lee,
And Spaniard on Spaniard smites, and shatters, and yields; and we,
Ere battle begin, stand lords of the battle, acclaimed of the sea.

And the day sweeps round to the nightward; and heavy and hard the waves
Roll in on the herd of the hurtling galleons; and masters and slaves
Reel blind in the grasp of the dark strong wind that shall dig their graves.

For the sepulchres hollowed and shaped of the wind in the swerve of the seas,
The graves that gape for their pasture, and laugh, thrilled through by the breeze,
The sweet soft merciless waters, await and are fain of these.

As the hiss of a Python heaving in menace of doom to be
They hear through the clear night round them, whose hours are as clouds that flee,
The whisper of tempest sleeping, the heave and the hiss of the sea.

But faith is theirs, and with faith are they girded and helmed and shod:
Invincible are they, almighty, elect for a sword and a rod;
Invincible even as their God is omnipotent, infinite, God.

In him is their strength, who have sworn that his glory shall wax not dim:
In his name are their war-ships hallowed as mightiest of all that swim:
The men that shall cope with these, and conquer, shall cast out him.

In him is the trust of their hearts; the desire of their eyes is he;
The light of their ways, made lightning for men that would fain be free:
Earth's hosts are with them, and with them is heaven: but with us is the sea.

V

I

And a day and a night pass over;
And the heart of their chief swells high;

For England, the warrior, the rover,
Whose banners on all winds fly,
Soul-stricken, he saith, by the shadow of death, holds off him, and draws not nigh.

And the wind and the dawn together
Make in from the gleaming east:
And fain of the wild glad weather
As famine is fain of feast,
And fain of the fight, forth sweeps in its might the host of the Lord's high priest.

And lightly before the breeze
The ships of his foes take wing:
Are they scattered, the lords of the seas?
Are they broken, the foes of the king?
And ever now higher as a mounting fire the hopes of the Spaniard spring.

And a windless night comes down:
And a breezeless morning, bright
With promise of praise to crown
The close of the crowning fight,
Leaps up as the foe's heart leaps, and glows with lustrous rapture of light.

And stinted of gear for battle
The ships of the sea's folk lie,
Unwarlike, herded as cattle,
Six miles from the foeman's eye
That fastens as flame on the sight of them tame and offenceless, and ranged as to die.

Surely the souls in them quail,
They are stricken and withered at heart,
When in on them, sail by sail,
Fierce marvels of monstrous art,
Tower darkening on tower till the sea-winds cower crowds down as to hurl them apart.

And the windless weather is kindly,
And comforts the host in these;
And their hearts are uplift in them blindly,
And blindly they boast at ease
That the next day's fight shall exalt them, and smite with destruction the lords of the seas.

II

And lightly the proud hearts prattle,
And lightly the dawn draws nigh,
The dawn of the doom of the battle
When these shall falter and fly;
No day more great in the roll of fate filled ever with fire the sky.

To fightward they go as to feastward,
And the tempest of ships that drive
Sets eastward ever and eastward,
Till closer they strain and strive;
And the shots that rain on the hulls of Spain are as thunders afire and alive.

And about them the blithe sea smiles
And flashes to windward and lee
Round capes and headlands and isles
That heed not if war there be;
Round Sark, round Wight, green jewels of light in the ring of the golden sea.

But the men that within them abide
Are stout of spirit and stark
As rocks that repel the tide,
As day that repels the dark;
And the light bequeathed from their swords unsheathed shines lineal on Wight and on Sark.

And eastward the storm sets ever,
The storm of the sails that strain
And follow and close and sever
And lose and return and gain;
And English thunder divides in sunder the holds of the ships of Spain.

Southward to Calais, appalled
And astonished, the vast fleet veers;
And the skies are shrouded and palled,
But the moonless midnight hears
And sees how swift on them drive and drift strange flames that the darkness fears.

They fly through the night from shoreward,
Heart-stricken till morning break,
And ever to scourge them forward
Drives down on them England's Drake,
And hurls them in as they hurtle and spin and stagger, with storm to wake.

VI

I

And now is their time come on them. For eastward they drift and reel,
With the shallows of Flanders ahead, with destruction and havoc at heel,
With God for their comfort only, the God whom they serve; and here
Their Lord, of his great loving-kindness, may revel and make good cheer;
Though ever his lips wax thirstier with drinking, and hotter the lusts in him swell;
For he feeds the thirst that consumes him with blood, and his winepress fumes with the reek of hell.

II

Fierce noon beats hard on the battle; the galleons that loom to the lee
Bow down, heel over, uplifting their shelterless hulls from the sea:
From scuppers aspirt with blood, from guns dismounted and dumb,
The signs of the doom they looked for, the loud mute witnesses come.
They press with sunset to seaward for comfort: and shall not they find it there?
O servants of God most high, shall his winds not pass you by, and his waves not spare?

III

The wings of the south-west wind are widened; the breath of his fervent lips,
More keen than a sword's edge, fiercer than fire, falls full on the plunging ships.
The pilot is he of their northward flight, their stay and their steersman he;
A helmsman clothed with the tempest, and girdled with strength to constrain the sea.
And the host of them trembles and quails, caught fast in his hand as a bird in the toils;
For the wrath and the joy that fulfil him are mightier than man's, whom he slays and spoils.
And vainly, with heart divided in sunder, and labour of wavering will,
The lord of their host takes counsel with hope if haply their star shine still,
If haply some light be left them of chance to renew and redeem the fray;
But the will of the black south-wester is lord of the councils of war to-day.
One only spirit it quells not, a splendour undarkened of chance or time;
Be the praise of his foes with Oquendo for ever, a name as a star sublime.
But here what aid in a hero's heart, what help in his hand may be?
For ever the dark wind whitens and blackens the hollows and heights of the sea,
And galley by galley, divided and desolate, founders; and none takes heed,
Nor foe nor friend, if they perish; forlorn, cast off in their uttermost need,
They sink in the whelm of the waters, as pebbles by children from shoreward hurled,
In the North Sea's waters that end not, nor know they a bourn but the bourn of the world.
Past many a secure unavailable harbour, and many a loud stream's mouth,
Past Humber and Tees and Tyne and Tweed, they fly, scourged on from the south,
And torn by the scourge of the storm-wind that smites as a harper smites on a lyre,
And consumed of the storm as the sacrifice loved of their God is consumed with fire,
And devoured of the darkness as men that are slain in the fires of his love are devoured,
And deflowered of their lives by the storms, as by priests is the spirit of life deflowered.
For the wind, of its godlike mercy, relents not, and hounds them ahead to the north,
With English hunters at heel, till now is the herd of them past the Forth,
All huddled and hurtled seaward; and now need none wage war upon these,
Nor huntsmen follow the quarry whose fall is the pastime sought of the seas.
Day upon day upon day confounds them, with measureless mists that swell,
With drift of rains everlasting and dense as the fumes of ascending hell.
The visions of priest and of prophet beholding his enemies bruised of his rod
Beheld but the likeness of this that is fallen on the faithful, the friends of God.
Northward, and northward, and northward they stagger and shudder and swerve and flit,
Dismantled of masts and of yards, with sails by the fangs of the storm-wind split.

But north of the headland whose name is Wrath, by the wrath or the ruth of the sea,
They are swept or sustained to the westward, and drive through the rollers aloof to the lee.
Some strive yet northward for Iceland, and perish: but some through the storm-hewn straits
That sunder the Shetlands and Orkneys are borne of the breath which is God's or fate's:
And some, by the dawn of September, at last give thanks as for stars that smile,
For the winds have swept them to shelter and sight of the cliffs of a Catholic isle.
Though many the fierce rocks feed on, and many the merciless heretic slays,
Yet some that have laboured to land with their treasure are trustful, and give God praise.
And the kernes of murderous Ireland, athirst with a greed everlasting of blood,
Unslakable ever with slaughter and spoil, rage down as a ravening flood,
To slay and to flay of their shining apparel their brethren whom shipwreck spares;
Such faith and such mercy, such love and such manhood, such hands and such hearts are theirs.
Short shrift to her foes gives England, but shorter doth Ireland to friends; and worse
Fare they that came with a blessing on treason than they that come with a curse.
Hacked, harried, and mangled of axes and skenes, three thousand naked and dead
Bear witness of Catholic Ireland, what sons of what sires at her breasts are bred.
Winds are pitiful, waves are merciful, tempest and storm are kind:
The waters that smite may spare, and the thunder is deaf, and the lightning is blind:
Of these perchance at his need may a man, though they know it not, yet find grace;
But grace, if another be hardened against him, he gets not at this man's face.
For his ear that hears and his eye that sees the wreck and the wail of men,
And his heart that relents not within him, but hungers, are like as the wolf's in his den.
Worthy are these to worship their master, the murderous Lord of lies,
Who hath given to the pontiff his servant the keys of the pit and the keys of the skies.
Wild famine and red-shod rapine are cruel, and bitter with blood are their feasts;
But fiercer than famine and redder than rapine the hands and the hearts of priests.
God, God bade these to the battle; and here, on a land by his servants trod,
They perish, a lordly blood-offering, subdued by the hands of the servants of God.
These also were fed of his priests with faith, with the milk of his word and the wine;
These too are fulfilled with the spirit of darkness that guided their quest divine.
And here, cast up from the ravening sea on the mild land's merciful breast,
This comfort they find of their fellows in worship; this guerdon is theirs of their quest.
Death was captain, and doom was pilot, and darkness the chart of their way;
Night and hell had in charge and in keeping the host of the foes of day.
Invincible, vanquished, impregnable, shattered, a sign to her foes of fear,
A sign to the world and the stars of laughter, the fleet of the Lord lies here.
Nay, for none may declare the place of the ruin wherein she lies;
Nay, for none hath beholden the grave whence never a ghost shall rise.
The fleet of the foemen of England hath found not one but a thousand graves;
And he that shall number and name them shall number by name and by tale the waves.

VII

I

Sixtus, Pope of the Church whose hope takes flight for heaven to dethrone the sun,
Philip, king that wouldst turn our spring to winter, blasted, appalled, undone,

Prince and priest, let a mourner's feast give thanks to God for your conquest won.

England's heel is upon you: kneel, O priest, O prince, in the dust, and cry,
"Lord, why thus? art thou wroth with us whose faith was great in thee, God most high?
Whence is this, that the serpent's hiss derides us? Lord, can thy pledged word lie?

"God of hell, are its flames that swell quenched now for ever, extinct and dead?
Who shall fear thee? or who shall hear the word thy servants who feared thee said?
Lord, art thou as the dead gods now, whose arm is shortened, whose rede is read?

"Yet we thought it was not for nought thy word was given us, to guard and guide:
Yet we deemed that they had not dreamed who put their trust in thee. Hast thou lied?
God our Lord, was the sacred sword we drew not drawn on thy Church's side?

"England hates thee as hell's own gates; and England triumphs, and Rome bows down:
England mocks at thee; England's rocks cast off thy servants to drive and drown:
England loathes thee; and fame betroths and plights with England her faith for crown.

"Spain clings fast to thee; Spain, aghast with anguish, cries to thee; where art thou?
Spain puts trust in thee; lo, the dust that soils and darkens her prostrate brow!
Spain is true to thy service; who shall raise up Spain for thy service now?

"Who shall praise thee, if none may raise thy servants up, nor affright thy foes?
Winter wanes, and the woods and plains forget the likeness of storms and snows:
So shall fear of thee fade even here: and what shall follow thee no man knows."

Lords of night, who would breathe your blight on April's morning and August's noon,
God your Lord, the condemned, the abhorred, sinks hellward, smitten with deathlike swoon:
Death's own dart in his hateful heart now thrills, and night shall receive him soon.

God the Devil, thy reign of revel is here for ever eclipsed and fled:
God the Liar, everlasting fire lays hold at last on thee, hand and head:
God the Accurst, the consuming thirst that burns thee never shall here be fed.

II

England, queen of the waves whose green inviolate girdle enrings thee round,
Mother fair as the morning, where is now the place of thy foemen found?
Still the sea that salutes us free proclaims them stricken, acclaims thee crowned.

Times may change, and the skies grow strange with signs of treason and fraud and fear:
Foes in union of strange communion may rise against thee from far and near:
Sloth and greed on thy strength may feed as cankers waxing from year to year.

Yet, though treason and fierce unreason should league and lie and defame and smite,
We that know thee, how far below thee the hatred burns of the sons of night,
We that love thee, behold above thee the witness written of life in light.

Life that shines from thee shows forth signs that none may read not but eyeless foes:
Hate, born blind, in his abject mind grows hopeful now but as madness grows:
Love, born wise, with exultant eyes adores thy glory, beholds and glows.

Truth is in thee, and none may win thee to lie, forsaking the face of truth:
Freedom lives by the grace she gives thee, born again from thy deathless youth:
Faith should fail, and the world turn pale, wert thou the prey of the serpent's tooth.

Greed and fraud, unabashed, unawed, may strive to sting thee at heel in vain:
Craft and fear and mistrust may leer and mourn and murmur and plead and plain:
Thou art thou: and thy sunbright brow is hers that blasted the strength of Spain.

Mother, mother beloved, none other could claim in place of thee England's place:
Earth bears none that beholds the sun so pure of record, so clothed with grace:
Dear our mother, nor son nor brother is thine, as strong or as fair of face.

How shalt thou be abased? or how shall fear take hold of thy heart? of thine,
England, maiden immortal, laden with charge of life and with hopes divine?
Earth shall wither, when eyes turned hither behold not light in her darkness shine.

England, none that is born thy son, and lives, by grace of thy glory, free,
Lives and yearns not at heart and burns with hope to serve as he worships thee;
None may sing thee: the sea-wind's wing beats down our songs as it hails the sea.

TO A SEAMEW

When I had wings, my brother,
Such wings were mine as thine:
Such life my heart remembers
In all as wild Septembers
As this when life seems other,
Though sweet, than once was mine;
When I had wings, my brother,
Such wings were mine as thine.

Such life as thrills and quickens
The silence of thy flight,
Or fills thy note's elation
With lordlier exultation
Than man's, whose faint heart sickens
With hopes and fears that blight
Such life as thrills and quickens
The silence of thy flight.

Thy cry from windward clanging

Makes all the cliffs rejoice;
Though storm clothe seas with sorrow,
Thy call salutes the morrow;
While shades of pain seem hanging
Round earth's most rapturous voice,
Thy cry from windward clanging
Makes all the cliffs rejoice.

We, sons and sires of seamen,
Whose home is all the sea,
What place man may, we claim it;
But thine—whose thought may name it?
Free birds live higher than freemen,
And gladlier ye than we—
We, sons and sires of seamen,
Whose home is all the sea.

For you the storm sounds only
More notes of more delight
Than earth's in sunniest weather:
When heaven and sea together
Join strengths against the lonely
Lost bark borne down by night,
For you the storm sounds only
More notes of more delight.

With wider wing, and louder
Long clarion-call of joy,
Thy tribe salutes the terror
Of darkness, wild as error,
But sure as truth, and prouder
Than waves with man for toy;
With wider wing, and louder
Long clarion-call of joy.

The wave's wing spreads and flutters,
The wave's heart swells and breaks;
One moment's passion thrills it,
One pulse of power fulfils it
And ends the pride it utters
When, loud with life that quakes,
The wave's wing spreads and flutters,
The wave's heart swells and breaks.

But thine and thou, my brother,
Keep heart and wing more high
Than aught may scare or sunder;
The waves whose throats are thunder

Fall hurtling each on other,
And triumph as they die;
But thine and thou, my brother,
Keep heart and wing more high.

More high than wrath or anguish,
More strong than pride or fear,
The sense or soul half hidden
In thee, for us forbidden,
Bids thee nor change nor languish,
But live thy life as here,
More high than wrath or anguish,
More strong than pride or fear.

We are fallen, even we, whose passion
On earth is nearest thine;
Who sing, and cease from flying;
Who live, and dream of dying:
Grey time, in time's grey fashion,
Bids wingless creatures pine:
We are fallen, even we, whose passion
On earth is nearest thine.

The lark knows no such rapture,
Such joy no nightingale,
As sways the songless measure
Wherein thy wings take pleasure:
Thy love may no man capture,
Thy pride may no man quail;
The lark knows no such rapture,
Such joy no nightingale.

And we, whom dreams embolden,
We can but creep and sing
And watch through heaven's waste hollow
The flight no sight may follow
To the utter bourne beholden
Of none that lack thy wing:
And we, whom dreams embolden,
We can but creep and sing.

Our dreams have wings that falter,
Our hearts bear hopes that die;
For thee no dream could better
A life no fears may fetter,
A pride no care can alter,
That wots not whence or why
Our dreams have wings that falter,

Our hearts bear hopes that die.

With joy more fierce and sweeter
Than joys we deem divine
Their lives, by time untarnished,
Are girt about and garnished,
Who match the wave's full metre
And drink the wind's wild wine
With joy more fierce and sweeter
Than joys we deem divine.

Ah, well were I for ever,
Wouldst thou change lives with me,
And take my song's wild honey,
And give me back thy sunny
Wide eyes that weary never,
And wings that search the sea;
Ah, well were I for ever,
Wouldst thou change lives with me.

Beachy Head: September 1886.

PAN AND THALASSIUS

A LYRICAL IDYL

THALASSIUS, PAN

PAN
O sea-stray, seed of Apollo,
What word wouldst thou have with me?
My ways thou wast fain to follow
Or ever the years hailed thee
Man.

Now
If August brood on the valleys,
If satyrs laugh on the lawns,
What part in the wildwood alleys
Hast thou with the fleet-foot fauns—
Thou?

See!
Thy feet are a man's—not cloven
Like these, not light as a boy's:
The tresses and tendrils inwoven

That lure us, the lure of them cloys
Thee.

Us
The joy of the wild woods never
Leaves free of the thirst it slakes:
The wild love throbs in us ever
That burns in the dense hot brakes
Thus.

Life,
Eternal, passionate, awless,
Insatiable, mutable, dear,
Makes all men's law for us lawless:
We strive not: how should we fear
Strife?

We,
The birds and the bright winds know not
Such joys as are ours in the mild
Warm woodland; joys such as grow not
In waste green fields of the wild
Sea.

No;
Long since, in the world's wind veering,
Thy heart was estranged from me:
Sweet Echo shall yield thee not hearing:
What have we to do with thee?
Go.

THALASSIUS
Ay!
Such wrath on thy nostril quivers
As once in Sicilian heat
Bade herdsmen quail, and the rivers
Shrank, leaving a path for thy feet
Dry?

Nay,
Low down in the hot soft hollow
Too snakelike hisses thy spleen:
"O sea-stray, seed of Apollo!"
What ill hast thou heard or seen?
Say.

Man

Knows well, if he hears beside him
The snarl of thy wrath at noon,
What evil may soon betide him,
Or late, if thou smite not soon,
Pan.

Me
The sound of thy flute, that flatters
The woods as they smile and sigh,
Charmed fast as it charms thy satyrs,
Can charm no faster than I
Thee.

Fast
Thy music may charm the splendid
Wide woodland silence to sleep
With sounds and dreams of thee blended
And whispers of waters that creep
Past.

Here
The spell of thee breathes and passes
And bids the heart in me pause,
Hushed soft as the leaves and the grasses
Are hushed if the storm's foot draws
Near.

Yet
The panic that strikes down strangers
Transgressing thy ways unaware
Affrights not me nor endangers
Through dread of thy secret snare
Set.

PAN
Whence
May man find heart to deride me?
Who made his face as a star
To shine as a God's beside me?
Nay, get thee away from us, far
Hence.

THALASSIUS
Then
Shall no man's heart, as he raises
A hymn to thy secret head,

Wax great with the godhead he praises:
Thou, God, shalt be like unto dead
Men.

PAN
Grace
I take not of men's thanksgiving,
I crave not of lips that live;
They die, and behold, I am living,
While they and their dead Gods give
Place.

THALASSIUS
Yea:
Too lightly the words were spoken
That mourned or mocked at thee dead:
But whose was the word, the token,
The song that answered and said
Nay?

PAN
Whose
But mine, in the midnight hidden,
Clothed round with the strength of night
And mysteries of things forbidden
For all but the one most bright
Muse?

THALASSIUS
Hers
Or thine, O Pan, was the token
That gave back empire to thee
When power in thy hands lay broken
As reeds that quake if a bee
Stirs?

PAN
Whom
Have I in my wide woods need of?
Urania's limitless eyes
Behold not mine end, though they read of
A word that shall speak to the skies
Doom.

THALASSIUS
She
Gave back to thee kingdom and glory,
And grace that was thine of yore,
And life to thy leaves, late hoary
As weeds cast up from the hoar
Sea.

Song
Can bid faith shine as the morning
Though light in the world be none:
Death shrinks if her tongue sound warning,
Night quails, and beholds the sun
Strong.

PAN
Night
Bare rule over men for ages
Whose worship wist not of me
And gat but sorrows for wages,
And hardly for tears could see
Light.

Call
No more on the starry presence
Whose light through the long dark swam:
Hold fast to the green world's pleasance:
For I that am lord of it am
All.

THALASSIUS
God,
God Pan, from the glad wood's portal
The breaths of thy song blow sweet:
But woods may be walked in of mortal
Man's thought, where never thy feet
Trod.

Thine
All secrets of growth and of birth are,
All glories of flower and of tree,
Wheresoever the wonders of earth are;
The words of the spell of the sea
Mine.

A BALLAD OF BATH

Like a queen enchanted who may not laugh or weep,
Glad at heart and guarded from change and care like ours,
Girt about with beauty by days and nights that creep
Soft as breathless ripples that softly shoreward sweep,
Lies the lovely city whose grace no grief deflowers.
Age and grey forgetfulness, time that shifts and veers,
Touch not thee, our fairest, whose charm no rival nears,
Hailed as England's Florence of one whose praise gives grace,
Landor, once thy lover, a name that love reveres:
Dawn and noon and sunset are one before thy face.

Dawn whereof we know not, and noon whose fruit we reap,
Garnered up in record of years that fell like flowers,
Sunset liker sunrise along the shining steep
Whence thy fair face lightens, and where thy soft springs leap,
Crown at once and gird thee with grace of guardian powers
Loved of men beloved of us, souls that fame inspheres,
All thine air hath music for him who dreams and hears;
Voices mixed of multitudes, feet of friends that pace,
Witness why for ever, if heaven's face clouds or clears,
Dawn and noon and sunset are one before thy face.

Peace hath here found harbourage mild as very sleep:
Not the hills and waters, the fields and wildwood bowers,
Smile or speak more tenderly, clothed with peace more deep,
Here than memory whispers of days our memories keep
Fast with love and laughter and dreams of withered hours.
Bright were these as blossom of old, and thought endears
Still the fair soft phantoms that pass with smiles or tears,
Sweet as roseleaves hoarded and dried wherein we trace
Still the soul and spirit of sense that lives and cheers:
Dawn and noon and sunset are one before thy face.

City lulled asleep by the chime of passing years,
Sweeter smiles thy rest than the radiance round thy peers;
Only love and lovely remembrance here have place.
Time on thee lies lighter than music on men's ears;
Dawn and noon and sunset are one before thy face.

IN A GARDEN

Baby, see the flowers!
　　—Baby sees
　　　Fairer things than these,
Fairer though they be than dreams of ours.

Baby, hear the birds!
　　—Baby knows
　　　Better songs than those,
Sweeter though they sound than sweetest words.

Baby, see the moon!
　　—Baby's eyes
　　　Laugh to watch it rise,
Answering light with love and night with noon.

Baby, hear the sea!
　　—Baby's face
　　　Takes a graver grace,
Touched with wonder what the sound may be.

Baby, see the star!
　　—Baby's hand
　　　Opens, warm and bland,
Calm in claim of all things fair that are.

Baby, hear the bells!
　　—Baby's head
　　　Bows, as ripe for bed,
Now the flowers curl round and close their cells.

Baby, flower of light,
　　Sleep, and see
　　　Brighter dreams than we,
Till good day shall smile away good night.

A RHYME

Babe, if rhyme be none
For that sweet small word
Babe, the sweetest one
Ever heard,

Right it is and meet
Rhyme should keep not true
Time with such a sweet
Thing as you.

Meet it is that rhyme
Should not gain such grace:
What is April's prime
To your face?

What to yours is May's
Rosiest smile? what sound
Like your laughter sways
All hearts round?

None can tell in metre
Fit for ears on earth
What sweet star grew sweeter
At your birth.

Wisdom doubts what may be:
Hope, with smile sublime,
Trusts: but neither, baby,
Knows the rhyme.

Wisdom lies down lonely;
Hope keeps watch from far;
None but one seer only
Sees the star.

Love alone, with yearning
Heart for astrolabe,
Takes the star's height, burning
O'er the babe.

BABY-BIRD

Baby-bird, baby-bird,
Ne'er a song on earth
May be heard, may be heard,
Rich as yours in mirth.

All your flickering fingers,
All your twinkling toes,
Play like light that lingers
Till the clear song close.

Baby-bird, baby-bird,
Your grave majestic eyes
Like a bird's warbled words

Speak, and sorrow dies.

Sorrow dies for love's sake,
Love grows one with mirth,
Even for one white dove's sake,
Born a babe on earth.

Baby-bird, baby-bird,
Chirping loud and long,
Other birds hush their words,
Hearkening toward your song.

Sweet as spring though it ring,
Full of love's own lures,
Weak and wrong sounds their song,
Singing after yours.

Baby-bird, baby-bird,
The happy heart that hears
Seems to win back within
Heaven, and cast out fears.

Earth and sun seem as one
Sweet light and one sweet word
Known of none here but one,
Known of one sweet bird.

OLIVE

I

Who may praise her?
Eyes where midnight shames the sun,
Hair of night and sunshine spun,
Woven of dawn's or twilight's loom,
Radiant darkness, lustrous gloom,
Godlike childhood's flowerlike bloom,
None may praise aright, nor sing
Half the grace wherewith like spring
Love arrays her.

II

Love untold
Sings in silence, speaks in light

Shed from each fair feature, bright
Still from heaven, whence toward us, now
Nine years since, she deigned to bow
Down the brightness of her brow,
Deigned to pass through mortal birth:
Reverence calls her, here on earth,
Nine years old.

III

Love's deep duty,
Even when love transfigured grows
Worship, all too surely knows
How, though love may cast out fear,
Yet the debt divine and dear
Due to childhood's godhead here
May by love of man be paid
Never; never song be made
Worth its beauty.

IV

Nought is all
Sung or said or dreamed or thought
Ever, set beside it; nought
All the love that man may give—
Love whose prayer should be, "Forgive!"
Heaven, we see, on earth may live;
Earth can thank not heaven, we know,
Save with songs that ebb and flow,
Rise and fall.

V

No man living,
No man dead, save haply one
Now gone homeward past the sun,
Ever found such grace as might
Tune his tongue to praise aright
Children, flowers of love and light,
Whom our praise dispraises: we
Sing, in sooth, but not as he
Sang thanksgiving.

VI

Hope that smiled,
Seeing her new-born beauty, made
Out of heaven's own light and shade,
Smiled not half so sweetly: love,
Seeing the sun, afar above,
Warm the nest that rears the dove,
Sees, more bright than moon or sun,
All the heaven of heavens in one
Little child.

VII

Who may sing her?
Wings of angels when they stir
Make no music worthy her:
Sweeter sound her shy soft words
Here than songs of God's own birds
Whom the fire of rapture girds
Round with light from love's face lit;
Hands of angels find no fit
Gifts to bring her.

VIII

Babes at birth
Wear as raiment round them cast,
Keep as witness toward their past,
Tokens left of heaven; and each,
Ere its lips learn mortal speech,
Ere sweet heaven pass on pass reach,
Bears in undiverted eyes
Proof of unforgotten skies
Here on earth.

IX

Quenched as embers
Quenched with flakes of rain or snow
Till the last faint flame burns low,
All those lustrous memories lie
Dead with babyhood gone by:
Yet in her they dare not die:
Others, fair as heaven is, yet,

Now they share not heaven, forget:
She remembers.

A WORD WITH THE WIND

Lord of days and nights that hear thy word of wintry warning,
Wind, whose feet are set on ways that none may tread,
Change the nest wherein thy wings are fledged for flight by morning,
Change the harbour whence at dawn thy sails are spread.
Not the dawn, ere yet the imprisoning night has half released her,
More desires the sun's full face of cheer, than we,
Well as yet we love the strength of the iron-tongued north-easter,
Yearn for wind to meet us as we front the sea.
All thy ways are good, O wind, and all the world should fester,
Were thy fourfold godhead quenched, or stilled thy strife:
Yet the waves and we desire too long the deep south-wester,
Whence the waters quicken shoreward, clothed with life.
Yet the field not made for ploughing save of keels nor harrowing
Save of storm-winds lies unbrightened by thy breath:
Banded broad with ruddy samphire glow the sea-banks narrowing
Westward, while the sea gleams chill and still as death.
Sharp and strange from inland sounds thy bitter note of battle,
Blown between grim skies and waters sullen-souled,
Till the baffled seas bear back, rocks roar and shingles rattle,
Vexed and angered and anhungered and acold.
Change thy note, and give the waves their will, and all the measure,
Full and perfect, of the music of their might,
Let it fill the bays with thunderous notes and throbs of pleasure,
Shake the shores with passion, sound at once and smite.
Sweet are even the mild low notes of wind and sea, but sweeter
Sounds the song whose choral wrath of raging rhyme
Bids the shelving shoals keep tune with storm's imperious metre,
Bids the rocks and reefs respond in rapturous chime.
Sweet the lisp and lulling whisper and luxurious laughter,
Soft as love or sleep, of waves whereon the sun
Dreams, and dreams not of the darkling hours before nor after,
Winged with cloud whose wrath shall bid love's day be done.
Yet shall darkness bring the awakening sea a lordlier lover,
Clothed with strength more amorous and more strenuous will,
Whence her heart of hearts shall kindle and her soul recover
Sense of love too keen to lie for love's sake still.
Let thy strong south-western music sound, and bid the billows
Brighten, proud and glad to feel thy scourge and kiss
Sting and soothe and sway them, bowed as aspens bend or willows,
Yet resurgent still in breathless rage of bliss.
All to-day the slow sleek ripples hardly bear up shoreward,

Charged with sighs more light than laughter, faint and fair,
Like a woodland lake's weak wavelets lightly lingering forward,
Soft and listless as the slumber-stricken air.
Be the sunshine bared or veiled, the sky superb or shrouded,
Still the waters, lax and languid, chafed and foiled,
Keen and thwarted, pale and patient, clothed with fire or clouded,
Vex their heart in vain, or sleep like serpents coiled.
Thee they look for, blind and baffled, wan with wrath and weary,
Blown for ever back by winds that rock the bird:
Winds that seamews breast subdue the sea, and bid the dreary
Waves be weak as hearts made sick with hope deferred.
Let thy clarion sound from westward, let the south bear token
How the glories of thy godhead sound and shine:
Bid the land rejoice to see the land-wind's broad wings broken,
Bid the sea take comfort, bid the world be thine.
Half the world abhors thee beating back the sea, and blackening
Heaven with fierce and woful change of fluctuant form:
All the world acclaims thee shifting sail again, and slackening
Cloud by cloud the close-reefed cordage of the storm.
Sweeter fields and brighter woods and lordlier hills than waken
Here at sunrise never hailed the sun and thee:
Turn thee then, and give them comfort, shed like rain and shaken
Far as foam that laughs and leaps along the sea.

NEAP-TIDE

Far off is the sea, and the land is afar:
The low banks reach at the sky,
Seen hence, and are heavenward high;
Though light for the leap of a boy they are,
And the far sea late was nigh.

The fair wild fields and the circling downs,
The bright sweet marshes and meads
All glorious with flowerlike weeds,
The great grey churches, the sea-washed towns,
Recede as a dream recedes.

The world draws back, and the world's light wanes,
As a dream dies down and is dead;
And the clouds and the gleams overhead
Change, and change; and the sea remains,
A shadow of dreamlike dread.

Wild, and woful, and pale, and grey,
A shadow of sleepless fear,

A corpse with the night for bier,
The fairest thing that beholds the day
Lies haggard and hopeless here.

And the wind's wings, broken and spent, subside;
And the dumb waste world is hoar,
And strange as the sea the shore;
And shadows of shapeless dreams abide
Where life may abide no more.

A sail to seaward, a sound from shoreward,
And the spell were broken that seems
To reign in a world of dreams
Where vainly the dreamer's feet make forward
And vainly the low sky gleams.

The sea-forsaken forlorn deep-wrinkled
Salt slanting stretches of sand
That slope to the seaward hand,
Were they fain of the ripples that flashed and twinkled
And laughed as they struck the strand?

As bells on the reins of the fairies ring
The ripples that kissed them rang,
The light from the sundawn sprang,
And the sweetest of songs that the world may sing
Was theirs when the full sea sang.

Now no light is in heaven; and now
Not a note of the sea-wind's tune
Rings hither: the bleak sky's boon
Grants hardly sight of a grey sun's brow—
A sun more sad than the moon.

More sad than a moon that clouds beleaguer
And storm is a scourge to smite,
The sick sun's shadowlike light
Grows faint as the clouds and the waves wax eager,
And withers away from sight.

The day's heart cowers, and the night's heart quickens:
Full fain would the day be dead
And the stark night reign in his stead:
The sea falls dumb as the sea-fog thickens
And the sunset dies for dread.

Outside of the range of time, whose breath
Is keen as the manslayer's knife

And his peace but a truce for strife,
Who knows if haply the shadow of death
May be not the light of life?

For the storm and the rain and the darkness borrow
But an hour from the suns to be,
But a strange swift passage, that we
May rejoice, who have mourned not to-day, to-morrow,
In the sun and the wind and the sea.

BY THE WAYSIDE

Summer's face was rosiest, skies and woods were mellow,
Earth had heaven to friend, and heaven had earth to fellow,
When we met where wooded hills and meadows meet.
Autumn's face is pale, and all her late leaves yellow,
Now that here again we greet.

Wan with years whereof this eightieth nears December,
Fair and bright with love, the kind old face I know
Shines above the sweet small twain whose eyes remember
Heaven, and fill with April's light this pale November,
Though the dark year's glass run low.

Like a rose whose joy of life her silence utters
When the birds are loud, and low the lulled wind mutters,
Grave and silent shines the boy nigh three years old.
Wise and sweet his smile, that falters not nor flutters,
Glows, and turns the gloom to gold.

Like the new-born sun's that strikes the dark and slays it,
So that even for love of light it smiles and dies,
Laughs the boy's blithe face whose fair fourth year arrays it
All with light of life and mirth that stirs and sways it
And fulfils the deep wide eyes.

Wide and warm with glowing laughter's exultation,
Full of welcome, full of sunbright jubilation,
Flash my taller friend's quick eyebeams, charged with glee;
But with softer still and sweeter salutation
Shine my smaller friend's on me.

Little arms flung round my bending neck, that yoke it
Fast in tender bondage, draw my face down too
Toward the flower-soft face whose dumb deep smiles invoke it;
Dumb, but love can read the radiant eyes that woke it,

Blue as June's mid heaven is blue.

How may men find refuge, how should hearts be shielded,
From the weapons thus by little children wielded,
When they lift such eyes as light this lustrous face—
Eyes that woke love sleeping unawares, and yielded
Love for love, a gift of grace,

Grace beyond man's merit, love that laughs, forgiving
Even the sin of being no more a child, nor worth
Trust and love that lavish gifts above man's giving,
Touch or glance of eyes and lips the sweetest living,
Fair as heaven and kind as earth?

NIGHT

I

FROM THE ITALIAN OF GIOVANNI STROZZI

Night, whom in shape so sweet thou here may'st see
Sleeping, was by an Angel sculptured thus
In marble, and since she sleeps hath life like us:
Thou doubt'st? Awake her: she will speak to thee.

II

FROM THE ITALIAN OF MICHELANGELO BUONARROTI

Sleep likes me well, and better yet to know
I am but stone. While shame and grief must be,
Good hap is mine, to feel not, nor to see:
Take heed, then, lest thou wake me: ah, speak low.

IN TIME OF MOURNING

"Return," we dare not as we fain
Would cry from hearts that yearn:
Love dares not bid our dead again
Return.

O hearts that strain and burn
As fires fast fettered burn and strain!

Bow down, lie still, and learn.

The heart that healed all hearts of pain
No funeral rites inurn:
Its echoes, while the stars remain,
Return.

May 1885.

THE INTERPRETERS

I

Days dawn on us that make amends for many
    Sometimes,
When heaven and earth seem sweeter even than any
    Man's rhymes.

Light had not all been quenched in France, or quelled
    In Greece,
Had Homer sung not, or had Hugo held
    His peace.

Had Sappho's self not left her word thus long
    For token,
The sea round Lesbos yet in waves of song
    Had spoken.

II

And yet these days of subtler air and finer
    Delight,
When lovelier looks the darkness, and diviner
    The light—

The gift they give of all these golden hours,
    Whose urn
Pours forth reverberate rays or shadowing showers
    In turn—

Clouds, beams, and winds that make the live day's track
    Seem living—
What were they did no spirit give them back
    Thanksgiving?

III

Dead air, dead fire, dead shapes and shadows, telling
    Time nought;
Man gives them sense and soul by song, and dwelling
    In thought.

In human thought their being endures, their power
    Abides:
Else were their life a thing that each light hour
    Derides.

The years live, work, sigh, smile, and die, with all
    They cherish;
The soul endures, though dreams that fed it fall
    And perish.

IV

In human thought have all things habitation;
    Our days
Laugh, lower, and lighten past, and find no station
    That stays.

But thought and faith are mightier things than time
    Can wrong,
Made splendid once with speech, or made sublime
    By song.

Remembrance, though the tide of change that rolls
    Wax hoary,
Gives earth and heaven, for song's sake and the soul's,
    Their glory.

July 16, 1885.

THE RECALL

Return, they cry, ere yet your day
Set, and the sky grow stern:
Return, strayed souls, while yet ye may
Return.

But heavens beyond us yearn;

Yea, heights of heaven above the sway
Of stars that eyes discern.

The soul whose wings from shoreward stray
Makes toward her viewless bourne
Though trustless faith and unfaith say,
Return.

BY TWILIGHT

If we dream that desire of the distance above us
Should be fettered by fear of the shadows that seem,
If we wake, to be nought, but to hate or to love us
If we dream,

Night sinks on the soul, and the stars as they gleam
Speak menace or mourning, with tongues to reprove us
That we deemed of them better than terror may deem.

But if hope may not lure us, if fear may not move us,
Thought lightens the darkness wherein the supreme
Pure presence of death shall assure us, and prove us
If we dream.

A BABY'S EPITAPH

April made me: winter laid me here away asleep.
Bright as Maytime was my daytime; night is soft and deep:
Though the morrow bring forth sorrow, well are ye that weep.

Ye that held me dear beheld me not a twelvemonth long:
All the while ye saw me smile, ye knew not whence the song
Came that made me smile, and laid me here, and wrought you wrong.

Angels, calling from your brawling world one undefiled,
Homeward bade me, and forbade me here to rest beguiled:
Here I sleep not: pass, and weep not here upon your child.

ON THE DEATH OF SIR HENRY TAYLOR

Fourscore and five times has the gradual year
Risen and fulfilled its days of youth and eld

Since first the child's eyes opening first beheld
Light, who now leaves behind to help us here
Light shed from song as starlight from a sphere
Serene as summer; song whose charm compelled
The sovereign soul made flesh in Artevelde
To stand august before us and austere,
Half sad with mortal knowledge, all sublime
With trust that takes no taint from change or time,
Trust in man's might of manhood. Strong and sage,
Clothed round with reverence of remembering hearts,
He, twin-born with our nigh departing age,
Into the light of peace and fame departs.

IN MEMORY OF JOHN WILLIAM INCHBOLD

Farewell: how should not such as thou fare well,
Though we fare ill that love thee, and that live,
And know, whate'er the days wherein we dwell
May give us, thee again they will not give?

Peace, rest, and sleep are all we know of death,
And all we dream of comfort: yet for thee,
Whose breath of life was bright and strenuous breath,
We think the change is other than we see.

The seal of sleep set on thine eyes to-day
Surely can seal not up the keen swift light
That lit them once for ever. Night can slay
None save the children of the womb of night.

The fire that burns up dawn to bring forth noon
Was father of thy spirit: how shouldst thou
Die as they die for whom the sun and moon
Are silent? Thee the darkness holds not now:

Them, while they looked upon the light, and deemed
That life was theirs for living in the sun,
The darkness held in bondage: and they dreamed,
Who knew not that such life as theirs was none.

To thee the sun spake, and the morning sang
Notes deep and clear as life or heaven: the sea
That sounds for them but wild waste music rang
Notes that were lost not when they rang for thee.

The mountains clothed with light and night and change,

The lakes alive with wind and cloud and sun,
Made answer, by constraint sublime and strange,
To the ardent hand that bade thy will be done.

We may not bid the mountains mourn, the sea
That lived and lightened from thine hand again
Moan, as of old would men that mourned as we
A man beloved, a man elect of men,

A man that loved them. Vain, divine and vain,
The dream that touched with thoughts or tears of ours
The spirit of sense that lives in sun and rain,
Sings out in birds, and breathes and fades in flowers.

Not for our joy they live, and for our grief
They die not. Though thine eye be closed, thine hand
Powerless as mine to paint them, not a leaf
In English woods or glades of Switzerland

Falls earlier now, fades faster. All our love
Moves not our mother's changeless heart, who gives
A little light to eyes and stars above,
A little life to each man's heart that lives.

A little life to heaven and earth and sea,
To stars and souls revealed of night and day,
And change, the one thing changeless: yet shall she
Cease too, perchance, and perish. Who shall say?

Our mother Nature, dark and sweet as sleep,
And strange as life and strong as death, holds fast,
Even as she holds our hearts alive, the deep
Dumb secret of her first-born births and last.

But this, we know, shall cease not till the strife
Of nights and days and fears and hopes find end;
This, through the brief eternities of life,
Endures, and calls from death a living friend;

The love made strong with knowledge, whence confirmed
The whole soul takes assurance, and the past
(So by time's measure, not by memory's, termed)
Lives present life, and mingles first with last.

I, now long since thy guest of many days,
Who found thy hearth a brother's, and with thee
Tracked in and out the lines of rolling bays
And banks and gulfs and reaches of the sea—

Deep dens wherein the wrestling water sobs
And pants with restless pain of refluent breath
Till all the sunless hollow sounds and throbs
With ebb and flow of eddies dark as death—

I know not what more glorious world, what waves
More bright with life,—if brighter aught may live
Than those that filled and fled their tidal caves—
May now give back the love thou hast to give.

Tintagel, and the long Trebarwith sand,
Lone Camelford, and Boscastle divine
With dower of southern blossom, bright and bland
Above the roar of granite-baffled brine,

Shall hear no more by joyous night or day
From downs or causeways good to rove and ride
Or feet of ours or horse-hoofs urge their way
That sped us here and there by tower and tide.

The headlands and the hollows and the waves,
For all our love, forget us: where I am
Thou art not: deeper sleeps the shadow on graves
Than in the sunless gulf that once we swam.

Thou hast swum too soon the sea of death: for us
Too soon, but if truth bless love's blind belief
Faith, born of hope and memory, says not thus:
And joy for thee for me should mean not grief.

And joy for thee, if ever soul of man
Found joy in change and life of ampler birth
Than here pens in the spirit for a span,
Must be the life that doubt calls death on earth.

For if, beyond the shadow and the sleep,
A place there be for souls without a stain,
Where peace is perfect, and delight more deep
Than seas or skies that change and shine again,

There none of all unsullied souls that live
May hold a surer station: none may lend
More light to hope's or memory's lamp, nor give
More joy than thine to those that called thee friend.

Yea, joy from sorrow's barren womb is born
When faith begets on grief the godlike child:

As midnight yearns with starry sense of morn
In Arctic summers, though the sea wax wild,

So love, whose name is memory, thrills at heart,
Remembering and rejoicing in thee, now
Alive where love may dream not what thou art
But knows that higher than hope or love art thou.

"Whatever heaven, if heaven at all may be,
Await the sacred souls of good men dead,
There, now we mourn who loved him here, is he,"
So, sweet and stern of speech, the Roman said,

Erect in grief, in trust erect, and gave
His deathless dead a deathless life even here
Where day bears down on day as wave on wave
And not man's smile fades faster than his tear.

Albeit this gift be given not me to give,
Nor power be mine to break time's silent spell,
Not less shall love that dies not while I live
Bid thee, beloved in life and death, farewell.

NEW YEAR'S DAY

New Year, be good to England. Bid her name
Shine sunlike as of old on all the sea:
Make strong her soul: set all her spirit free:
Bind fast her homeborn foes with links of shame
More strong than iron and more keen than flame:
Seal up their lips for shame's sake: so shall she
Who was the light that lightened freedom be,
For all false tongues, in all men's eyes the same.

O last-born child of Time, earth's eldest lord,
God undiscrowned of godhead, who for man
Begets all good and evil things that live,
Do thou, his new-begotten son, implored
Of hearts that hope and fear not, make thy span
Bright with such light as history bids thee give.

Jan. 1, 1889.

TO SIR RICHARD F. BURTON

(ON HIS TRANSLATION OF "THE ARABIAN NIGHTS")

Westward the sun sinks, grave and glad; but far
Eastward, with laughter and tempestuous tears,
Cloud, rain, and splendour as of orient spears,
Keen as the sea's thrill toward a kindling star,
The sundawn breaks the barren twilight's bar
And fires the mist and slays it. Years on years
Vanish, but he that hearkens eastward hears
Bright music from the world where shadows are.

Where shadows are not shadows. Hand in hand
A man's word bids them rise and smile and stand
And triumph. All that glorious orient glows
Defiant of the dusk. Our twilight land
Trembles; but all the heaven is all one rose,
Whence laughing love dissolves her frosts and snows.

NELL GWYN

Sweet heart, that no taint of the throne or the stage
Could touch with unclean transformation, or alter
To the likeness of courtiers whose consciences falter
At the smile or the frown, at the mirth or the rage,
Of a master whom chance could inflame or assuage,
Our Lady of Laughter, invoked in no psalter,
Adored of no faithful that cringe and that palter,
Praise be with thee yet from a hag-ridden age.

Our Lady of Pity thou wast: and to thee
All England, whose sons are the sons of the sea,
Gives thanks, and will hear not if history snarls
When the name of the friend of her sailors is spoken;
And thy lover she cannot but love—by the token
That thy name was the last on the lips of King Charles.

CALIBAN ON ARIEL

"His backward voice is to utter foul speeches and to detract"

The tongue is loosed of that most lying slave,
Whom stripes may move, not kindness. Listen: "Lo,
The real god of song, Lord Stephano,

That's a brave god, if ever god were brave,
And bears celestial liquor: but," the knave
(A most ridiculous monster) howls, "we know
From Ariel's lips what springs of poison flow,
The chicken-heart blasphemer! Hear him rave!"

Thou poisonous slave, got by the devil himself
Upon thy wicked dam, the witch whose name
Is darkness, and the sun her eyes' offence,
Though hell's hot sewerage breed no loathlier elf,
Men cry not shame upon thee, seeing thy shame
So perfect: they but bid thee—"Hag-seed, hence!"

THE WEARY WEDDING

O daughter, why do ye laugh and weep,
One with another?
For woe to wake and for will to sleep,
Mother, my mother.

But weep ye winna the day ye wed,
One with another.
For tears are dry when the springs are dead,
Mother, my mother.

Too long have your tears run down like rain,
One with another.
For a long love lost and a sweet love slain,
Mother, my mother.

Too long have your tears dripped down like dew,
One with another.
For a knight that my sire and my brethren slew,
Mother, my mother.

Let past things perish and dead griefs lie,
One with another.
O fain would I weep not, and fain would I die,
Mother, my mother.

Fair gifts we give ye, to laugh and live,
One with another.
But sair and strange are the gifts I give,
Mother, my mother.

And what will ye give for your father's love?

One with another.
Fruits full few and thorns enough,
Mother, my mother.

And what will ye give for your mother's sake?
One with another.
Tears to brew and tares to bake,
Mother, my mother.

And what will ye give your sister Jean?
One with another.
A bier to build and a babe to wean,
Mother, my mother.

And what will ye give your sister Nell?
One with another.
The end of life and beginning of hell,
Mother, my mother.

And what will ye give your sister Kate?
One with another.
Earth's door and hell's gate,
Mother, my mother.

And what will ye give your brother Will?
One with another.
Life's grief and world's ill,
Mother, my mother.

And what will ye give your brother Hugh?
One with another.
A bed of turf to turn into,
Mother, my mother.

And what will ye give your brother John?
One with another.
The dust of death to feed upon,
Mother, my mother.

And what will ye give your bauld bridegroom?
One with another.
A barren bed and an empty room,
Mother, my mother.

And what will ye give your bridegroom's friend?
One with another.
A weary foot to the weary end,
Mother, my mother.

And what will ye give your blithe bridesmaid?
One with another.
Grief to sew and sorrow to braid,
Mother, my mother.

And what will ye drink the day ye're wed?
One with another.
But ae drink of the wan well-head,
Mother, my mother.

And whatten a water is that to draw?
One with another.
We maun draw thereof a', we maun drink thereof a',
Mother, my mother.

And what shall ye pu' where the well rins deep?
One with another.
Green herb of death, fine flower of sleep,
Mother, my mother.

Are there ony fishes that swim therein?
One with another.
The white fish grace, and the red fish sin,
Mother, my mother.

Are there ony birds that sing thereby?
One with another.
O when they come thither they sing till they die,
Mother, my mother.

Is there ony draw-bucket to that well-head?
One with another.
There's a wee well-bucket hangs low by a thread,
Mother, my mother.

And whatten a thread is that to spin?
One with another.
It's green for grace, and it's black for sin,
Mother, my mother.

And what will ye strew on your bride-chamber floor?
One with another.
But one strewing and no more,
Mother, my mother.

And whatten a strewing shall that one be?
One with another.

The dust of earth and sand of the sea,
Mother, my mother.

And what will ye take to build your bed?
One with another.
Sighing and shame and the bones of the dead,
Mother, my mother.

And what will ye wear for your wedding gown?
One with another.
Grass for the green and dust for the brown,
Mother, my mother.

And what will ye wear for your wedding lace?
One with another.
A heavy heart and a hidden face,
Mother, my mother.

And what will ye wear for a wreath to your head?
One with another.
Ash for the white and blood for the red,
Mother, my mother.

And what will ye wear for your wedding ring?
One with another.
A weary thought for a weary thing,
Mother, my mother.

And what shall the chimes and the bell-ropes play?
One with another.
A weary tune on a weary day,
Mother, my mother.

And what shall be sung for your wedding song?
One with another.
A weary word of a weary wrong,
Mother, my mother.

The world's way with me runs back,
One with another,
Wedded in white and buried in black,
Mother, my mother.

The world's day and the world's night,
One with another,
Wedded in black and buried in white,
Mother, my mother.

The world's bliss and the world's teen,
One with another,
It's red for white and it's black for green,
Mother, my mother.

The world's will and the world's way,
One with another,
It's sighing for night and crying for day,
Mother, my mother.

The world's good and the world's worth,
One with another,
It's earth to flesh and it's flesh to earth,
Mother, my mother.

When she came out at the kirkyard gate,
(One with another)
The bridegroom's mother was there in wait.
(Mother, my mother.)

O mother, where is my great green bed,
(One with another)
Silk at the foot and gold at the head,
Mother, my mother?

Yea, it is ready, the silk and the gold,
One with another.
But line it well that I lie not cold,
Mother, my mother.

She laid her cheek to the velvet and vair,
One with another;
She laid her arms up under her hair.
(Mother, my mother.)

Her gold hair fell through her arms fu' low,
One with another:
Lord God, bring me out of woe!
(Mother, my mother.)

Her gold hair fell in the gay reeds green,
One with another:
Lord God, bring me out of teen!
(Mother, my mother.)

O mother, where is my lady gone?
(One with another.)
In the bride-chamber she makes sore moan:

(Mother, my mother.)

Her hair falls over the velvet and vair,
(One with another)
Her great soft tears fall over her hair.
(Mother, my mother.)

When he came into the bride's chamber,
(One with another)
Her hands were like pale yellow amber.
(Mother, my mother.)

Her tears made specks in the velvet and vair,
(One with another)
The seeds of the reeds made specks in her hair.
(Mother, my mother.)

He kissed her under the gold on her head;
(One with another)
The lids of her eyes were like cold lead.
(Mother, my mother.)

He kissed her under the fall of her chin;
(One with another)
There was right little blood therein.
(Mother, my mother.)

He kissed her under her shoulder sweet;
(One with another)
Her throat was weak, with little heat.
(Mother, my mother.)

He kissed her down by her breast-flowers red,
One with another;
They were like river-flowers dead.
(Mother, my mother.)

What ails you now o' your weeping, wife?
(One with another.)
It ails me sair o' my very life.
(Mother, my mother.)

What ails you now o' your weary ways?
(One with another.)
It ails me sair o' my long life-days.
(Mother, my mother.)

Nay, ye are young, ye are over fair.

(One with another.)
Though I be young, what needs ye care?
(Mother, my mother.)

Nay, ye are fair, ye are over sweet.
(One with another.)
Though I be fair, what needs ye greet?
(Mother, my mother.)

Nay, ye are mine while I hold my life.
(One with another.)
O fool, will ye marry the worm for a wife?
(Mother, my mother.)

Nay, ye are mine while I have my breath.
(One with another.)
O fool, will ye marry the dust of death?
(Mother, my mother.)

Yea, ye are mine, we are handfast wed,
One with another.
Nay, I am no man's; nay, I am dead,
Mother, my mother.

THE WINDS

O weary fa' the east wind,
And weary fa' the west:
And gin I were under the wan waves wide
I wot weel wad I rest.

O weary fa' the north wind,
And weary fa' the south:
The sea went ower my good lord's head
Or ever he kissed my mouth.

Weary fa' the windward rocks,
And weary fa' the lee:
They might hae sunken sevenscore ships,
And let my love's gang free.

And weary fa' ye, mariners a',
And weary fa' the sea:
It might hae taken an hundred men,
And let my ae love be.

A LYKE-WAKE SONG

Fair of face, full of pride,
Sit ye down by a dead man's side.

Ye sang songs a' the day:
Sit down at night in the red worm's way.

Proud ye were a' day long:
Ye'll be but lean at evensong.

Ye had gowd kells on your hair:
Nae man kens what ye were.

Ye set scorn by the silken stuff:
Now the grave is clean enough.

Ye set scorn by the rubis ring:
Now the worm is a saft sweet thing.

Fine gold and blithe fair face,
Ye are come to a grimly place.

Gold hair and glad grey een,
Nae man kens if ye have been.

A REIVER'S NECK-VERSE

Some die singing, and some die swinging,
And weel mot a' they be:
Some die playing, and some die praying,
And I wot sae winna we, my dear,
And I wot sae winna we.

Some die sailing, and some die wailing,
And some die fair and free:
Some die flyting, and some die fighting,
But I for a fause love's fee, my dear,
But I for a fause love's fee.

Some die laughing, and some die quaffing,
And some die high on tree:
Some die spinning, and some die sinning,
But faggot and fire for ye, my dear,

Faggot and fire for ye.

Some die weeping, and some die sleeping,
And some die under sea:
Some die ganging, and some die hanging,
And a twine of a tow for me, my dear,
A twine of a tow for me.

THE WITCH-MOTHER

"O where will ye gang to and where will ye sleep,
Against the night begins?"
"My bed is made wi' cauld sorrows,
My sheets are lined wi' sins.

"And a sair grief sitting at my foot,
And a sair grief at my head;
And dule to lay me my laigh pillows,
And teen till I be dead.

"And the rain is sair upon my face,
And sair upon my hair;
And the wind upon my weary mouth,
That never may man kiss mair.

"And the snow upon my heavy lips,
That never shall drink nor eat;
And shame to cledding, and woe to wedding,
And pain to drink and meat.

"But woe be to my bairns' father,
And ever ill fare he:
He has tane a braw bride hame to him,
Cast out my bairns and me."

"And what shall they have to their marriage meat
This day they twain are wed?"
"Meat of strong crying, salt of sad sighing,
And God restore the dead."

"And what shall they have to their wedding wine
This day they twain are wed?"
"Wine of weeping, and draughts of sleeping,
And God raise up the dead."

She's tane her to the wild woodside,

Between the flood and fell:
She's sought a rede against her need
Of the fiend that bides in hell.

She's tane her to the wan burnside,
She's wrought wi' sang and spell:
She's plighted her soul for doom and dole
To the fiend that bides in hell.

She's set her young son to her breast,
Her auld son to her knee:
Says, "Weel for you the night, bairnies,
And weel the morn for me."

She looked fu' lang in their een, sighing,
And sair and sair grat she:
She has slain her young son at her breast,
Her auld son at her knee.

She's sodden their flesh wi' saft water,
She's mixed their blood with wine:
She's tane her to the braw bride-house,
Where a' were boun' to dine.

She poured the red wine in his cup,
And his een grew fain to greet:
She set the baked meats at his hand,
And bade him drink and eat.

Says, "Eat your fill of your flesh, my lord,
And drink your fill of your wine;
For a' thing's yours and only yours
That has been yours and mine."

Says, "Drink your fill of your wine, my lord,
And eat your fill of your bread:
I would they were quick in my body again,
Or I that bare them dead."

He struck her head frae her fair body,
And dead for grief he fell:
And there were twae mair sangs in heaven,
And twae mair sauls in hell.

THE BRIDE'S TRAGEDY

"The wind wears roun', the day wears doun,
The moon is grisly grey;
There's nae man rides by the mirk muirsides,
Nor down the dark Tyne's way."
In, in, out and in,
Blaws the wind and whirls the whin.

"And winna ye watch the night wi' me,
And winna ye wake the morn?
Foul shame it were that your ae mither
Should brook her ae son's scorn."
In, in, out and in,
Blaws the wind and whirls the whin.

"O mither, I may not sleep nor stay,
My weird is ill to dree;
For a fause faint lord of the south seaboard
Wad win my bride of me."
In, in, out and in,
Blaws the wind and whirls the whin.

"The winds are strang, and the nights are lang,
And the ways are sair to ride:
And I maun gang to wreak my wrang,
And ye maun bide and bide."
In, in, out and in,
Blaws the wind and whirls the whin.

"Gin I maun bide and bide, Willie,
I wot my weird is sair:
Weel may ye get ye a light love yet,
But never a mither mair."
In, in, out and in,
Blaws the wind and whirls the whin.

"O gin the morrow be great wi' sorrow,
The wyte be yours of a':
But though ye slay me that haud and stay me,
The weird ye will maun fa'."
In, in, out and in,
Blaws the wind and whirls the whin.

When cocks were crawing and day was dawing,
He's boun' him forth to ride:
And the ae first may he's met that day
Was fause Earl Robert's bride.
In, in, out and in,
Blaws the wind and whirls the whin.

O blithe and braw were the bride-folk a',
But sad and saft rade she;
And sad as doom was her fause bridegroom,
But fair and fain was he.
In, in, out and in,
Blaws the wind and whirls the whin.

"And winna ye bide, sae saft ye ride,
And winna ye speak wi' me?
For mony's the word and the kindly word
I have spoken aft wi' thee."
In, in, out and in,
Blaws the wind and whirls the whin.

"My lamp was lit yestreen, Willie,
My window-gate was wide:
But ye camena nigh me till day came by me
And made me not your bride."
In, in, out and in,
Blaws the wind and whirls the whin.

He's set his hand to her bridle-rein,
He's turned her horse away:
And the cry was sair, and the wrath was mair,
And fast and fain rode they.
In, in, out and in,
Blaws the wind and whirls the whin.

But when they came by Chollerford,
I wot the ways were fell;
For broad and brown the spate swang down,
And the lift was mirk as hell.
In, in, out and in,
Blaws the wind and whirls the whin.

"And will ye ride yon fell water,
Or will ye bide for fear?
Nae scathe ye'll win o' your father's kin,
Though they should slay me here."
In, in, out and in,
Blaws the wind and whirls the whin.

"I had liefer ride yon fell water,
Though strange it be to ride,
Than I wad stand on the fair green strand
And thou be slain beside."
In, in, out and in,

Blaws the wind and whirls the whin.

"I had liefer swim yon wild water,
Though sair it be to bide,
Than I wad stand at a strange man's hand,
To be a strange man's bride."
In, in, out and in,
Blaws the wind and whirls the whin.

"I had liefer drink yon dark water,
Wi' the stanes to make my bed,
And the faem to hide me, and thou beside me,
Than I wad see thee dead."
In, in, out and in,
Blaws the wind and whirls the whin.

He's kissed her twice, he's kissed her thrice,
On cheek and lip and chin:
He's wound her rein to his hand again,
And lightly they leapt in.
In, in, out and in,
Blaws the wind and whirls the whin.

Their hearts were high to live or die,
Their steeds were stark of limb:
But the stream was starker, the spate was darker,
Than man might live and swim.
In, in, out and in,
Blaws the wind and whirls the whin.

The first ae step they strode therein,
It smote them foot and knee:
But ere they wan to the mid water
The spate was as the sea.
In, in, out and in,
Blaws the wind and whirls the whin.

But when they wan to the mid water,
It smote them hand and head:
And nae man knows but the wave that flows
Where they lie drowned and dead.
In, in, out and in,
Blaws the wind and whirls the whin.

A JACOBITE'S FAREWELL

1716

There's nae mair lands to tyne, my dear,
And nae mair lives to gie:
Though a man think sair to live nae mair,
There's but one day to die.

For a' things come and a' days gane,
What needs ye rend your hair?
But kiss me till the morn's morrow,
Then I'll kiss ye nae mair.

O lands are lost and life's losing,
And what were they to gie?
Fu' mony a man gives all he can,
But nae man else gives ye.

Our king wons ower the sea's water,
And I in prison sair:
But I'll win out the morn's morrow,
And ye'll see me nae mair.

A JACOBITE'S EXILE

1746

The weary day rins down and dies,
The weary night wears through:
And never an hour is fair wi' flower,
And never a flower wi' dew.

I would the day were night for me,
I would the night were day:
For then would I stand in my ain fair land,
As now in dreams I may.

O lordly flow the Loire and Seine,
And loud the dark Durance:
But bonnier shine the braes of Tyne
Than a' the fields of France;
And the waves of Till that speak sae still
Gleam goodlier where they glance.

O weel were they that fell fighting
On dark Drumossie's day:
They keep their hame ayont the faem,

And we die far away.

O sound they sleep, and saft, and deep,
But night and day wake we;
And ever between the sea-banks green
Sounds loud the sundering sea.

And ill we sleep, sae sair we weep,
But sweet and fast sleep they;
And the mool that haps them roun' and laps them
Is e'en their country's clay;
But the land we tread that are not dead
Is strange as night by day.

Strange as night in a strange man's sight,
Though fair as dawn it be:
For what is here that a stranger's cheer
Should yet wax blithe to see?

The hills stand steep, the dells lie deep,
The fields are green and gold:
The hill-streams sing, and the hill-sides ring,
As ours at home of old.

But hills and flowers are nane of ours,
And ours are oversea:
And the kind strange land whereon we stand,
It wotsna what were we
Or ever we came, wi' scathe and shame,
To try what end might be.

Scathe, and shame, and a waefu' name,
And a weary time and strange,
Have they that seeing a weird for dreeing
Can die, and cannot change.

Shame and scorn may we thole that mourn,
Though sair be they to dree:
But ill may we bide the thoughts we hide,
Mair keen than wind and sea.

Ill may we thole the night's watches,
And ill the weary day:
And the dreams that keep the gates of sleep,
A waefu' gift gie they;
For the sangs they sing us, the sights they bring us,
The morn blaws all away.

On Aikenshaw the sun blinks braw,
The burn rins blithe and fain:
There's nought wi' me I wadna gie
To look thereon again.

On Keilder-side the wind blaws wide;
There sounds nae hunting-horn
That rings sae sweet as the winds that beat
Round banks where Tyne is born.

The Wansbeck sings with all her springs,
The bents and braes give ear;
But the wood that rings wi' the sang she sings
I may not see nor hear;
For far and far thae blithe burns are,
And strange is a' thing near.

The light there lightens, the day there brightens,
The loud wind there lives free:
Nae light comes nigh me or wind blaws by me
That I wad hear or see.

But O gin I were there again,
Afar ayont the faem,
Cauld and dead in the sweet saft bed
That haps my sires at hame!

We'll see nae mair the sea-banks fair,
And the sweet grey gleaming sky,
And the lordly strand of Northumberland,
And the goodly towers thereby:
And none shall know but the winds that blow
The graves wherein we lie.

THE TYNESIDE WIDOW

There's mony a man loves land and life,
Loves life and land and fee;
And mony a man loves fair women,
But never a man loves me, my love,
But never a man loves me.

O weel and weel for a' lovers,
I wot weel may they be;
And weel and weel for a' fair maidens,
But aye mair woe for me, my love,

But aye mair woe for me.

O weel be wi' you, ye sma' flowers,
Ye flowers and every tree;
And weel be wi' you, a' birdies,
But teen and tears wi' me, my love,
But teen and tears wi' me.

O weel be yours, my three brethren,
And ever weel be ye;
Wi' deeds for doing and loves for wooing,
But never a love for me, my love,
But never a love for me.

And weel be yours, my seven sisters,
And good love-days to see,
And long life-days and true lovers,
But never a day for me, my love,
But never a day for me.

Good times wi' you, ye bauld riders,
By the hieland and the lee;
And by the leeland and by the hieland
It's weary times wi' me, my love,
It's weary times wi' me.

Good days wi' you, ye good sailors,
Sail in and out the sea;
And by the beaches and by the reaches
It's heavy days wi' me, my love,
It's heavy days wi' me.

I had his kiss upon my mouth,
His bairn upon my knee;
I would my soul and body were twain,
And the bairn and the kiss wi' me, my love,
And the bairn and the kiss wi' me.

The bairn down in the mools, my dear,
O saft and saft lies she;
I would the mools were ower my head,
And the young bairn fast wi' me, my love,
And the young bairn fast wi' me.

The father under the faem, my dear,
O sound and sound sleeps he;
I would the faem were ower my face,
And the father lay by me, my love,

And the father lay by me.

I would the faem were ower my face,
Or the mools on my ee-bree;
And waking-time with a' lovers,
But sleeping-time wi' me, my love,
But sleeping-time wi' me.

I would the mools were meat in my mouth,
The saut faem in my ee;
And the land-worm and the water-worm
To feed fu' sweet on me, my love,
To feed fu' sweet on me.

My life is sealed with a seal of love,
And locked with love for a key;
And I lie wrang and I wake lang,
But ye tak' nae thought for me, my love,
But ye tak' nae thought for me.

We were weel fain of love, my dear,
O fain and fain were we;
It was weel with a' the weary world,
But O, sae weel wi' me, my love,
But O, sae weel wi' me.

We were nane ower mony to sleep, my dear,
I wot we were but three;
And never a bed in the weary world
For my bairn and my dear and me, my love,
For my bairn and my dear and me.

DEDICATION

The years are many, the changes more,
Since wind and sun on the wild sweet shore
Where Joyous Gard stands stark by the sea
With face as bright as in years of yore

Shone, swept, and sounded, and laughed for glee
More deep than a man's or a child's may be,
On a day when summer was wild and glad,
And the guests of the wind and the sun were we.

The light that lightens from seasons clad
With darkness now, is it glad or sad?

Not sad but glad should it shine, meseems,
On eyes yet fain of the joy they had.

For joy was there with us; joy that gleams
And murmurs yet in the world of dreams
Where thought holds fast, as a constant warder,
The days when I rode by moors and streams,

Reining my rhymes into buoyant order
Through honied leagues of the northland border.
Though thought or memory fade, and prove
A faithless keeper, a thriftless hoarder,

One landmark never can change remove,
One sign can the years efface not. Love,
More strong than death or than doubt may be,
Treads down their strengths, and abides above.

Yea, change and death are his servants: we,
Whom love of the dead links fast, though free,
May smile as they that beheld the dove
Bear home her signal across the sea.

Algernon Charles Swinburne – A Short Biography

Algernon Charles Swinburne was born at 7 Chester Street, Grosvenor Place, in London, on April 5th, 1837. He was the eldest of six children born to Captain Charles Henry Swinburne and Lady Jane Henrietta, daughter of the 3rd Earl of Ashburnham, a wealthy Northumbrian family.

Swinburne spent his early years at East Dene in Bonchurch, on the Isle of Wight. As a child, Swinburne was nervous and frail, but also imbued with a nervous energy and fearlessness almost to the point of recklessness.

He was schooled at Eton College from 1849 to 1853. It was here that he first began to write poetry. He excelled at languages and whilst still at Eton won first prizes in both French and Italian.

From Eton he moved to Oxford where he attended at Balliol College from 1856. Here he met friends to whom he became closely attached, among them Dante Gabriel Rossetti, William Morris and Edward Burne-Jones, who in 1857, were painting their Arthurian murals on the walls of the Oxford Union. At Oxford Swinburne was mentored by Benjamin Jowett, the master of Balliol College, who recognised his poetic talent and, intervening on his behalf, tried to keep him from being expelled when he celebrated the Italian patriot Orsini, and his failed attempt on the life of Napoleon III in 1858. Swinburne had to leave the Universcity for a few months due to this but returned in May, 1860 but never received a degree.

Summers were usually spent at Capheaton Hall in Northumberland, the house of his grandfather, Sir John Swinburne, 6th Baronet, who had a famous library and was himself President of the Literary and Philosophical Society in Newcastle upon Tyne.

Swinburne proudly considered himself a native of Northumberland and this is reflected in poems such as the intensely patriotic 'Northumberland' and 'Grace Darling'. He enjoyed riding across the moors and was, it was said, a daring horseman, as he moved 'through honeyed leagues of the northland border', as he remembered the Scottish border in his Recollections.

In the period from 1857 to 1860, Swinburne was one of a number of Pre-Raphaelite's who visited and became part of Lady Pauline Trevelyan's intellectual circle at Wallington Hall, a few miles west of Morpeth in Northumberland.

After leaving college, he moved to London and began his career in earnest as well as becoming a constant visitor to the Rossetti's house. To Rossetti Swinburne was his 'little Northumbrian friend', an affectionate reference to Swinburne's small stature—a mere five foot four. Whatever Swinburne lacked in height he made up for in poetic talent. However, with the burden of such great talent came the unveiling of a dark side that was to cause him pain and would, at times, threaten his very existence with all manner of self-inflicted pains through drink, drugs and sado-machoism.

In 1860 Swinburne published two verse dramas; The Queen Mother and Rosamond but it would not be until 1865 that Swinburne would achieve literary success with Atalanta in Calydon.

In 1861, Swinburne visited Menton on the French Riviera to recover from the effects of yet another period of excess use of alcohol, staying at the Villa Laurenti. From Menton, Swinburne then travelled on to Italy, where he journeyed widely.

After Elizabeth Rossetti's death from suicide in 1862, he and Rossetti moved to Tudor House at 16 Cheyne Walk in Chelsea. The stories that survive from his year with Rossetti are typical Swinburne. In one, Rossetti once had to tell him to keep down the noise — he and a boyfriend had been sliding naked down the bannisters and disturbing Rossetti's painting. He took a sardonic delight in what the critic and biographer, Cecil Lang, calls "Algernonic exaggeration": When people began to talk scathingly about his homosexuality and other sexual proclivities, he circulated a story that he had engaged in pederasty and bestiality with a monkey — and then eaten it. How many of the stories were true and how many invented is unclear. Oscar Wilde called him "a braggart in matters of vice, who had done everything he could to convince his fellow citizens of his homosexuality and bestiality without being in the slightest degree a homosexual or a bestialiser."

In December 1862, Swinburne accompanied Scott and his guests on a trip to Tynemouth. Scott writes in his memoirs that, as they walked by the sea, Swinburne declaimed the as yet unpublished 'Hymn to Proserpine' and 'Laus Veneris' in his lilting intonation, while the waves 'were running the whole length of the long level sands towards Cullercoats and sounding like far-off acclamations'.

Swinburne possessed a curious combination of frail health and strength. He was small and slightly built, but an excellent swimmer and the first to climb Culver Cliff on the Isle of Wight. He had an extremely excitable disposition: people who met him described him as a "demoniac boy" who would go skipping about the room declaiming poetry at the top of his voice. In this as in many things, moderation was not the standard for him. Excess was. Once or twice he had fits, thought to be epileptic, in public; but he made this condition much worse by drinking past excess to unconsciousness. More than once he was delivered to the door in the small of the night, dead drunk. Throughout the 1860s and '70s he rode an alcoholic cycle of dissolution, collapse, drying out at home in the country, then returning to London where he would begin the cycle all over again.

His mania for masochism, particularly flagellation, most probably started in early childhood at Eton and was encouraged by his later friendships with Richard Monckton Milnes (one of Tennyson's fellow Apostles), who introduced him to the works of the Marquis de Sade, and Richard Burton, the Victorian explorer and adventurer. Swinburne was an alcoholic and algolagniac (a desire for sexual gratification through inflicting pain on oneself or others; sadomasochism). He found life difficult, unfulfilling but still his poetic talents pushed to the fore.

Although Swinburne continued to publish some works in periodicals in 1865 he was granted recognition by both public and critics with Atalanta in Calydon written in the style of a classical Greek tragedy.

There followed "Laus Veneris" and Poems and Ballads (1866), with their sexually charged passages, absolutely decadent for polite Victorian society, which were attacked all the more violently as a result. The poems written in homage of Sappho of Lesbos such as "Anactoria" and "Sapphics" were especially savaged. The volume also contained poems such as "The Leper," "Laus Veneris," and "St Dorothy" which evoke both Swinburne's and a general Victorian fascination with the Middle Ages, and are explicitly mediaeval in style, tone and construction. With its publication came instant notoriety. He was now identified with indecent and decadent themes and the precept of art for art's sake.

Swinburne's meeting in 1867 with his long-time hero Mazzini, the Italian patriot living in England in exile, was the beginning of a poetical journey that now became more serious and more engaged with serious thought, initially leading to the political poems in the volume Songs Before Sunrise.

Also in 1867 he was introduced to Adah Isaacs Menken, the American actress, poet and circus rider, whose main fame seemed to be riding naked on a horse (in fact she wore tight nude coloured clothing) for her performance in the melodrama Mazeppa (itself based on a poem by Lord Byron). Although they had a short affair Adah's quote implies that Swinburne was not ready for a relationship that did not involve some self-sabotage; "I can't make him understand that biting's no use."

In 1879, with Swinburne nearly dead from alcoholism and dissolution, his legal advisor Theodore Watts-Dunton took him in, and was gradually successful in getting him to adapt to a healthier lifestyle. Swinburne lived the rest of his life at Watts-Dunton's house. He saw less and less of his old bohemian friends, who thought him a prisoner at The Pines, but his growing deafness also accounts for some of his decreased sociability. By now Swinburne was 42, and was moving from a young man of rebelliousness to a figure of social respectability. It was said of Watts-Dunton that he saved the man and killed the poet.

It is clear that Swinburne had an addictive personality, and clearly incapable of moderation in his pursuit of any chosen vices. This, of course, would both nourish and perhaps sabotage his poetic career. His poetry follows the somewhat clichéd pattern of early flourish and later decline; indeed some of the fresher pieces in the second and third series of Poems and Ballads (published in 1878 and 1889) were actually written during his days at Oxford. Nevertheless, his last collection, A Channel Passage, has some beautiful poems, including "The Lake of Gaube."

He is best remembered as the supreme technician in metre, with a versatility which exceeds even Tennyson's, but which lacks a corresponding emotional range. His obsessions are not widely enough shared; and if he cannot shock us by the strangeness of his desires nor the shrillness of his anti-theistical exclamations, often what remains is not enough to fully engage with the audience.

Swinburne is considered a poet of the decadent school, although he perhaps professed to more vice than he actually indulged in to advertise his deviance. Common gossip of the time reported that he also had a deep crush on the explorer Sir Richard Francis Burton, despite the fact that Swinburne himself abhorred travel. Fact and fiction are easily absorbed by the other so are difficult to untangle even now.

Many critics consider his mastery of vocabulary, rhyme and metre impressive, although he has also been criticised for his florid style and word choices that only fit the rhyme scheme rather than contributing to the meaning of the piece. A. E. Housman, although a critic, had great praise for his rhyming ability: to Swinburne the sonnet was child's play: the task of providing four rhymes was not hard enough, and he wrote long poems in which each stanza required eight or ten rhymes, and wrote them so that he never seemed to be saying anything for the rhyme's sake.

Throughout his career Swinburne published literary criticism of great worth. His deep knowledge of world literatures contributed to a critical style rich in quotation, allusion, and comparison. He is particularly noted for discerning studies of Elizabethan dramatists and of many English and French poets and novelists. As well he was a noted essayist and wrote two novels.

Swinburne was nominated for the Nobel Prize in Literature every year from 1903 to 1907 and then again in 1909.

H.P. Lovecraft, the master of the dark side and a decent poet himself, considered Swinburne "the only real poet in either England or America after the death of Mr. Edgar Allan Poe."

Swinburne was also responsible for devising a poetic form called the roundel, a variation of the French Rondeau form. In 1883 he published A Century of Roundels with several of the roundels dedicated to Dante's sister, the poet Christina Georgina Rossetti. Swinburne wrote to Edward Burne-Jones in 1883: "I have got a tiny new book of songs or songlets, in one form and all manner of metres ... just coming out, of which Miss Rossetti has accepted the dedication. I hope you and Georgie [his wife Georgiana] will find something to like among a hundred poems of nine lines each, twenty-four of which are about babies or small children".

Opinions of the Roundel poems move between those who find them captivating and brilliant, to others who find them merely clever and contrived. One of them, A Baby's Death, was set to music by the English composer Sir Edward Elgar as the song "Roundel: The little eyes that never knew Light".

After the first Poems and Ballads, Swinburne's later poetry was devoted more to philosophy and politics, including the unification of Italy, particularly in the volume Songs before Sunrise. He did not stop writing love poetry entirely, indeed it was only in 1882 that his great epic-length poem, Tristram of Lyonesse, was published, its contents lyrical rather than shocking. His versification, and especially his rhyming technique, remain of high quality to the end.

Algernon Charles Swinburne died of influenza, at the Pines in London on April 10th, 1909 at the age of 72. He was buried at St. Boniface Church, Bonchurch on the Isle of Wight.

Algernon Charles Swinburne – A Concise Bibliography

Verse Drama
The Queen Mother (1860)
Rosamond (1860)
Chastelard (1865)
Bothwell (1874)
Mary Stuart (1881)
Marino Faliero (1885)
Locrine (1887)
The Sisters (1892)
Rosamund, Queen of the Lombards (1899)

Poetry
Atalanta in Calydon (1865)*
Poems and Ballads (1866)
Songs Before Sunrise (1871)
Songs of Two Nations (1875)
Erechtheus (1876)*
Poems and Ballads, Second Series (1878)
Songs of the Springtides (1880)
Studies in Song (1880)
The Heptalogia, or the Seven against Sense. A Cap with Seven Bells (1880)
Tristram of Lyonesse (1882)
A Dark Month & Other Poems
A Century of Roundels (1883)
A Midsummer Holiday and Other Poems (1884)
Poems and Ballads, Third Series (1889)
Astrophel and Other Poems (1894)
The Tale of Balen (1896)
A Channel Passage and Other Poems (1904)

*Although formally tragedies, Atlanta in Calydon and Erechtheus are traditionally included with his poetry.

Criticism
William Blake: A Critical Essay (1868, new edition 1906)
Under the Microscope (1872)
George Chapman: A Critical Essay (1875)
Essays and Studies (1875)
A Note on Charlotte Brontë (1877)
A Study of Shakespeare (1880)
A Study of Victor Hugo (1886)
A Study of Ben Johnson (1889)
Studies in Prose and Poetry (1894)

The Age of Shakespeare (1908)
Shakespeare (1909)

Major Collections
The Poems of Algernon Charles Swinburne, 6 vols. 1904.
The Tragedies of Algernon Charles Swinburne, 5 vols. 1905.
The Complete Works of Algernon Charles Swinburne, 20 vols. Bonchurch Edition. 1925-7.
The Swinburne Letters, 6 vols. 1959-62.